Also by Stuart Stevens

The Last Season

The Last Season

A Father, a Son, and a
Lifetime of College Football

Stuart Stevens

Alfred A. Knopf   New York   2015

THIS IS A BORZOI BOOK
PUBLISHED BY ALFRED A. KNOPF

www.aaknopf.com

Knopf, Borzoi Books, and the colophon are registered trademarks of
Penguin Random House LLC.

Stevens, Stuart.
The last season : a father, a son, and a lifetime of college football /
Stuart Stevens. — First United States Edition.
pages   cm
ISBN 978-0-385-35302-1 (hardcover; alk. paper);
ISBN 978-0-385-35344-1 (eBook)
1. Stevens, Stuart.   2. Fathers and sons—United States—Biography.
3. Football—United States—Anecdotes.   4. University of Mississippi—
Football.   I. Title.
GV939.S743A3 2015   796.3320973—dc23   2015003268

Jacket photograph by George Baier IV
Jacket design by Oliver Munday

Manufactured in the United States of America
First Edition

For all the wonderful teachers who taught me how
to read and tried to teach me to write

"There comes a time when every summer will have something of autumn about it."

—A. Bartlett Giamatti,
"The Green Fields of the Mind"

The Last Season

Prologue

It was the first Ole Miss game that season in Jackson, and I'd been looking forward to it all summer. I had an Ole Miss hat, sort of a cross between a baseball hat and a newsboy cap that I wore to bed most nights. I knew the names of every starting Rebel as though they were family members: the all-American quarterback Glynn Griffing; the running back Lou Guy; the fullback and linebacker Buck Randall. I knew them all. The way the radio announcers described them was how I thought of the Rebels: "rocket-armed" Griffing; "swivel-hipped" Guy; "bruising" Randall. They were like titles bestowed upon knights competing on fields of battle.

I was ten years old.

My parents had a party before most Ole Miss games in Jackson. My favorite was the party before the Arkansas Razorbacks game, which was always a "hog roast" with lots of great barbeque and a big pig. I loved the pig.

The opening home game of that 1962 season was against the Kentucky Wildcats. You can't roast a wildcat, but it was still a good party. They always had good parties.

The bootlegger came to the house before every party. Mississippi was the only state in the country that had not repealed Prohibition, so the entire state was dry and everybody had a bootlegger. Ours drove a pickup truck with cases of booze in the back. Not very discreet, but nobody really tried to hide bootlegging. The state tax collector even received a percentage of a bootlegger's tax. You could make a lot of money, and one famous candidate for the office, when asked how long he intended to serve, said, "I figure it will only take one term."

I liked our bootlegger. He was a friendly guy who always gave me an ice-cold Coke. Once I saw a pistol in the cab of his pickup, and I asked my father if he was a police officer. He laughed and said that he wasn't but he probably had a lot of friends who were.

The pregame parties always ended with a couple of the Ole Miss chants, "Hotty Toddy," and a dash for the stadium. For evening games, there would be an inevitable clothing ritual with my mother that played out with the predictability of a catechism.

"Take a coat. It's going to get cool."

"I've got a jacket." I held up the light Ole Miss Windbreaker that had been a birthday present the year before. I'd learned not to fight these things. Submission was inevitable, so best to make it speedy.

"Is that heavy enough? Shouldn't you wear that nice wool coat we got you for Christmas?"

The wool coat was the sort of thing that the lead character in *Sergeant Preston of the Yukon* wore in one of my favorite television shows. Unless the temperature plummeted seventy degrees, I knew I'd want to abandon it on the walk to Memorial Stadium, like heavy equipment on the German retreat from Stalingrad. I'd seen pictures of that in the *Life* magazine book of World War II that I kept in my room. Next to the Rebels, I was probably in love with World War II more than anything.

"I'm okay. Really, Mom. I've got a coat."

As he always did at some point, my father stepped in. "He's fine," he reassured her. Then he held up the overly warm coat he had slung over his arm as a talisman to head off the next round of antihypothermia suggestions.

My dad and I always went to Memorial Stadium the same way: he'd drive just a couple of miles to the parking lot of Bailey Junior High School, and we'd walk. My aunt taught at Bailey, and later it was where I went to school. It was a formidable-looking art deco structure that always reminded me, not in a positive way, of the Emerald City in *The Wizard of Oz*. It was about a mile to the stadium from our usual parking spot. I loved that last stretch. Dad and I would hold hands and talk about the different ways the Rebels were going to win. He usually wore a snazzy hat, and sometimes when the afternoon sun caught us just right, our shadows fell long and lean on the sidewalk, stretching his hat out in funny shapes that made me laugh. The walk never felt routine. Even from a distance, the band warming up the crowd always seemed impossibly loud. The roar probably had something to do with the sound being funneled by the structure and amplified through the crowd. But it might have been my imagination teased to a frenzy in anticipation.

Walking to the game wasn't like going to the Capri movie theater, our neighborhood favorite. Even if you didn't know what was going to happen in a movie, it had already been made. But the game was different. Nobody had made what was going to unfold. No one had any idea what was going to happen. We were walking to history. I imagined families all across the country huddled around radios and big cabinet televisions like the huge

Zenith in our living room, listening and watching what we were going to see for real. Going to the game seemed like being on the inside of the most important secret in the world.

I knew that my friends at school who didn't go to the game would ask over and over, "What was it like?" Some wouldn't want to believe that I had really been there. I always carried the ticket stubs with me for at least a week after a game.

On the way to the game, Confederate flags were everywhere, but that was normal. What would Rebel games be without Rebel flags? Cars drove by with guys and sometimes a girl holding flags and yelling, "Go to hell, Kentucky!"

I always loved the way the crowds got bigger the closer we got to the stadium. It was like seeing kids on the playground before the first day of school after the long summer. Not that I was friends with my fellow fans, or even knew more than a handful of them, but they were Rebel fans. We were Rebel fans. Perfect strangers would greet each other with "Hotty Toddy," and it was like a password into our special clubhouse.

But this time, my dad steered us clear of any large groups. There was a crowd in the parking lot shouting, "Hell no!" and even I could tell they were drunk.

At halftime, Ole Miss was ahead 7–0. But my father seemed uneasy, shaking his head and talking about how "sloppy" the team had played. One of my favorite players, Buck Randall, had scored, but the refs called it back on holding. "We should be killin' 'em," my dad told me, and I nodded solemnly.

As soon as the teams had headed to the locker room, Colonel Reb, the Ole Miss mascot, led out the world's largest Confederate flag, which seemed to cover the field, followed by the Ole Miss band wearing their standard uniforms of Confederate battle dress. This was the ritual of every Ole Miss game: Colonel Reb, the giant flag, and when the marching band finished its famous rendition of "Dixie," the crowd would rise as one to shout, "The South shall rise again!"

But tonight, the ritual changed. A podium was placed in the center of the field, and a man I had seen before but couldn't have named came out flanked by Mississippi highway patrolmen.

"It's Ross!" somebody shouted.

"Hey, Governor!"

Governor Ross Barnett looked old and addled. People were laughing. Someone handed us a leaflet with the words for a new Mississippi anthem. The band started playing the Ross Barnett campaign song that I'd heard on the radio many times, "Roll with Ross," but now the crowd was singing the new lyrics:

States may sing their songs of praise
With waving flags and hip-hoo-rays,
Let cymbals crash and let bells ring
'Cause here's one song I'm proud to sing:
Go, Mississippi, keep rolling along,
Go, Mississippi, you cannot go wrong,
Go, Mississippi, we're singing your song,
M-I-S-S-I-S-S-I-P-P-I!

A few people near us in the stands looked uncomfortable, but most were laughing and singing. My father pushed his hat back on his head and stared at the paper. I wanted to join in, of course, but his look told me not to.

Ross Barnett was now waving his arms like a conductor. The crowd tore into the next verse:

We will not yield an inch of any field.
Fix us another toddy, ain't yielding to nobody.
Ross is standing like Gibraltar, he shall never falter.
Ask us what we say, it's to hell with Bobby K.
Never shall our emblem go
From Colonel Rebel to Ole Black Joe.

That was more than enough for my father. "Time to go," he said and pulled on my hand. I assumed he meant time to get some hot dogs. I loved hot dogs. We started to move down our row toward an aisle. Barnett was bellowing, "I love Mississippi! I love Mississippi! I love her people! Our customs! I love and respect our heritage!"

The crowd had stopped laughing and cheered wildly.

When we got to the hot dog stands on the ground floor, I stopped because I thought it was hot dog time. My father walked ahead for a few steps, then came back. "Halftime hot dog?" he asked. He bought me one, but he didn't look happy.

"Aren't you getting one?"

"Not tonight," he said, and instead of turning to go back into the stadium, he motioned toward the exit. "Let's go home."

"Home?"

He looked at me and then rubbed his stomach. "I don't feel good. I ate too much at that party. We can listen to the second half at home." Then, when he saw me hesitating, he said, "There's peach cobbler left from the party."

I loved the cobbler. I took a big bite out of the hot dog, and we walked out. Ross Barnett was still shouting.

Twenty-four hours later, the Ole Miss campus was a war zone in the last battle of the Civil War, federal troops fighting southerners over integration. Two weeks after that, the United States and Russia would come close to war over nuclear missiles in Cuba. But for me, 1962 will always be most remembered as the year my father and I cheered as Ole Miss went undefeated and won the national championship. It's there, floating in memory, that perfect season in that most imperfect year.

There were other seasons, some good, some not so good, but always shared with my father. And then life's wheel began to spin, and days and nights spent in stadiums faded into the past.

Until one day I woke up at the age of sixty and realized that what I wanted most in the world was one more season. With my father and football and the Ole Miss Rebels. It didn't need to be a perfect season. One last season would be perfect enough.

1

The fortunate among us realize early that loss is the key in which much of life is played. I was a little late coming to this realization. My life and sense of self-worth had been constructed around a very simple paradigm: there was winning and there was losing and nothing gray in between. It was part of what I liked most about politics. For a while, when I won, I was happy. Over time, that slowly changed to the point where winning was the absence of pain more than some form of joy. What hadn't changed was the horrible self-loathing that came with losing. It wasn't abstract or remote but a depressing, long-lasting sort of funk when no food tasted good and the best days were still lousy ones. Even when I knew that a campaign had gone as well as could be expected and we'd lost because of larger forces, it offered little comfort.

This was terribly predictable and not in the least profound. I had maneuvered through life with basically the emotional construct of the homecoming game. When you came off the field and the scoreboard showed you had won, you had . . . won. And what could possibly be better than winning? Or worse than losing?

On election night 2012 as I was getting numbers from small courthouses around Ohio, I found myself starting to think more about loss. Not just the election loss and the moments ahead, when I would have to walk into a hotel suite with a man and his family I had come to care for deeply and tell them that we had failed. It was a larger sense of loss. As grim staffers kept pushing new pieces of paper into my hand with vote counts, I tried to focus on the next steps. You do that in a campaign. You process information, good or bad, and move forward. We were going to lose this campaign. I had lost before, though not often and never at this level. The secret of success as a political consultant is to work for candidates who were going to win anyway and not screw it up. I'd picked candidates well.

Walking to Mitt Romney's hotel room on election night, down a hallway that wasn't long enough, I found myself asking the sorts of probing questions that an industry of self-help experts argue are essential to a well-led life: When was the last time I'd really been happy? What was it that I really cared about in life? Those experts may tell you such riddles open a path to happiness, but I had long suspected that they were employed mostly by those who believe—really, really believe—that the love of their life is just waiting on Match.com. I couldn't remember ever asking myself questions like this on a night when we'd won. I suppose I'd always thought self-examination and introspection were what losers did instead of celebrating.

It had been a long campaign. I had turned sixty on a campaign plane a couple of weeks earlier, an event I'd made sure no one "celebrated." I hated birthdays, and the notion of a campaign plane party, with some cake purchased by an advance staffer and reporters hovering around tweeting photographs, made me want to hurl myself straight out an emergency door.

But it wasn't really me or my birthday I was thinking about; it was my father's. In six weeks or so, he would turn ninety-five.

Ninety-five is a pretty unimaginable number, but then turning sixty was a baffling notion as well. In the long hours after concession, waiting for the sun to come up to muddle through the inevitable awful day after, I suddenly realized I had an answer to one of the perennial campaign questions, "What do you plan to do after the race?" This had always been an easy question for me because, win or lose, I knew what I'd do: another campaign. I had never been interested in working in government of any sort and was confident I'd be terrible at the effort, even if it had appeal. I was one of those guys whose usefulness, if any, was in the taking of Baghdad, not the running of it.

But now I had a different sort of answer. I wanted to spend time with my mother and father while it was still possible. And I knew exactly how I wanted to do it.

When I was growing up, the ritual of going to Ole Miss football games had been one of those special connections that fortunate fathers and sons discover. We had stumbled onto this shared joy the first time my father brought me to a game and found it was a way of being close without seeming to work at it. We tried to keep that ritual alive as the usual forces fought to move us apart: college, jobs, and wider horizons to explore.

When I was honest with myself, and no doubt some of my frantic pace was a way of avoiding honest reflection, I didn't think anything I'd done in life had meant as much to me, or brought as much sheer joy, as the Saturdays spent down south in stadiums with my dad. I could have kept doing that over the years, made the effort to make sure my father and I had that special time together. But of course I hadn't. And he was never one to pressure me to do this or that. It just wasn't his style. He had never urged me to go to Ole Miss and become a lawyer, as he and his grandfather had done, or to live in the South. He'd been one of those fathers who were for what I was for.

But now it was suddenly clear that nothing was more important than getting back to those games with my dad. Everything else seemed stale and trite. All the goals I'd set for myself, that rushing around to gulp in more life like a buffet at closing time, none of that seemed to mean a thing compared with just walking with him through a dark stadium tunnel to share the perfection of the hundred yards, bathed in sunlight or the magical glow of the field lights, hovering over the stadium like a giant UFO. I didn't have to chase all over the world or put myself through the meat grinder of politics. I could just go back home, and it was there, waiting for me.

It may seem strange to some that football would be so connected to my sense of family and home, but I doubt many southerners will find it mystifying. When I was growing up in Mississippi, football, particularly college football, loomed so large it reduced most endeavors to vaguely silly pursuits, a variation on racewalking or croquet.

I thought of the simple rituals my dad and I had developed going to games together, losing ourselves in their pleasures. What did it mean that the first memory I had of holding my father's hand was going to the Ole Miss–Arkansas game at Jackson Memorial Stadium? It was a rickety old stadium not that far from our house. The parking lot was filled with insane Arkansas fans yelling, "Woo Pig Sooie!" I was terrified. Everyone seemed to know my father. He was wearing a sport coat and a hat, sort of like the one that Bear Bryant would later make famous. I was nine years old. When we got to the steps, he offered to carry me, but I wanted to walk because only little kids were carried. So we walked, slowly.

Years later, I found the ticket stubs in the back of a drawer in my childhood room. I still remember the score: Ole Miss 16, Arkansas 0.

I loved everything about it, of course: the crowd, the yelling, the messy hot dogs, and the whiff of violence that hung in the air like a mist. I was too young to understand the game, but that would change, and with it grew a deep love. Most of all, I loved feeling safe with my dad. Now at sixty, reeling from a shattering defeat, I missed the confidence and comfort that as a boy those moments had so effortlessly provided.

Dad with me and my sister, Riverside Park, Jackson

The games of my youth were huge spectacles: foggy nights in LSU's Tiger Stadium, hot afternoons at Jackson Memorial Stadium, long car drives to the hills of Arkansas to face the dreaded Razorbacks. We'd talk about the game all the way, and if we won, we'd talk about it all the way back. If we lost, mostly we rode in silence and played over and over in our heads what could have been, should have been. There came a time—I can't remember when exactly, and no doubt it was more gradual than sudden—when I realized it was being together with my father that I looked forward to as much as the game. When civil rights, Vietnam, and Watergate were ripping apart our country, my father and I could talk about anything by talking about nothing but football. It was a secret language that needed no translation. Those seasons had come and gone, and though we'd caught a game here or there and talked on the phone after a big, sweet moment like Ole Miss upsetting Tim Tebow and Florida, it didn't have the continuity of a real season. It was a casual drop by, not a shared passion that bound us together. But it didn't have to be that way. What was stopping us from grabbing one more season together? What was more valuable than a chance to spend time with my parents, to steal one more season?

And there'd be the games, those wonderful Saturdays that were always so perfect because they never were. Love of sports will always break your heart, but in doing so, it reminds us we have one. At this point in my life, that seemed like a worthy goal.

I flew to Charlotte and drove to Asheville, where my parents lived, on a hot summer day. The shortest way is west toward Spartanburg, South Carolina, but I like a slightly longer northern route through Hickory, North Carolina. Once I escaped from the suburbs of Charlotte, there was no city traffic, and soon the road began to tilt upward to the Smokies. I'd made this drive many times in the years since my parents moved to Asheville, and I always found the return reassuring.

My parents moved to Asheville because it was one of those places that always had a certain mystical tug for my mother. It was more than just mountains and Thomas Wolfe. For our family, and not a few Mississippians, North Carolina was a place to be envied. It was far enough north that summers were cooler and the schools the stuff of legend, but it was still part of a southerner's world. It was over the horizon but not beyond the Pillars of Hercules.

They had originally settled in a Methodist retirement community in Asheville. I thought it was great: organized and pleasant with someone to take care of everything. There was a large campus for the community, and their house was big and comfortable, with plenty of room in the basement for my bike and a big desk to write. But my mother never liked it. The uniformity of it wore on her, and compared with her touchstone of all that was aesthetically pleasing, New Orleans, it was one rabbit hutch of a house after another. So, inevitably, they left and moved to a condo in Asheville just minutes from a tennis club where my father at ninety-five still played. We had lived in one place—Piedmont Street in the Belhaven neighborhood of Jackson, Mississippi—from the time I was born until some time after I left college. Then it seems my parents, freed from kids, had succumbed to a long-suppressed peripatetic instinct. They sold the house and embarked on a succession of moves that ended for a longish stretch in Fairhope, Alabama. Along the way, there were apartments in New Orleans and one French Quarter renovation. My mother, who had mostly grown up in New Orleans, was never really happy without some connection to the city.

Now they divided their time between Asheville and New Orleans. My sister was not far away during the summers, west in the mountains in Cashiers, North Carolina, the rest of the year in Laurel, Mississippi. It was like this for many southerners; part of us longed to be elsewhere, but we could never quite make the break. I'd managed to pretend I'd left, but it was a sham; I'd always be not only a southerner but a Mississippian. It was like shaving my head to change hair color. It would always grow back the same.

The drive to Asheville was one more reenactment of the ritual I'd begun when I left home at fourteen to go to school in the far north of Virginia. But for the first time in a very long time, it wasn't just to drop by with a few moments to steal while the world waited at the door and the screen of my phone. This time I was here to talk about spending more time. It wasn't as if I were putting the world on hold. Now I wanted my world to revolve around those special Saturdays with my dad.

I pulled up in front of their one-story condominium, thinking about how I was going to put it to my parents that we spend the fall with the Ole Miss team. A large man, gray and old, really old, came out carrying a big garbage can. It took me a second to realize it was my father. He looked at me and smiled, and then I didn't feel sixty and he didn't seem ninety-five. I got out of the car. "What do you think about going to some Ole Miss games this year?"

2

Vanderbilt was the first game, in Nashville, an early game set to prime the pump for SEC football craziness. The year before, Ole Miss had lost to them in the final seconds. Both teams had charismatic young coaches who were in the middle of building new programs with great promise. It was easy to understand why it was being featured on television as the season's big opener.

In theory, driving from Asheville to Nashville is a simple matter. But travel with my family, even by car, has always been a complicated business, and my parents being eighty-six and ninety-five did not make it easier. The drive should take four and a half hours. The game started at 9:15 p.m., late because of the television schedule. The hotel was so close to the stadium they touted that some of the best seats for the game were from the rooms. "We should leave early," my mother said, "to beat the traffic."

"What traffic?" my father asked. "We're going through the mountains. There'll be more deer than cars. Anyway, we have all day. Game starts at 9:15 tonight."

"You don't know what will happen," my mother countered.

This was the kind of statement to which there really was no effective comeback. How could you argue, "Well, actually, I know exactly what will happen"? There was something reassuringly familiar about this travel routine. No matter how seemingly easy the journey, my mother would approach each as if she were running mission control for the first manned landing on Mars. Multiple alternatives would be explored and then planned in detail, like possible reentry sites in case of bad weather.

Outside their bedroom door was a growing pile of luggage. I had a bad feeling but had to ask, "What's this?"

"Don't be mean," my mother said. Then a bit more tentatively, "Do you think it will all fit?"

It took forever to pack the car. My parents had not bought new luggage since the middle of the last century; gathered together, it looked like the stuff you see homeless people pushing around in certain sad urban areas. Actually, it looked more like the belongings of a small convention of homeless people: a dozen small bags of various sorts stuffed with everything from shoes to pillows, tattered suitcases with broken zippers. And a lot of ripped plastic hang-up bags from various long-defunct clothing stores.

After a long struggle, we managed to get about two-thirds into the apartment-sized trunk of their old Toyota Avalon. As a tribute to Japanese technology, the car ran beautifully after more than 125,000 miles but was so battered and dented that it seemed to have been driven off the set of a *Mad Max* remake. My parents thought any bodywork was superficial and vain. As I struggled to fit the last of the bags and suitcases inside, I asked my mother, "Is all this stuff necessary?"

My mother paused and said thoughtfully, "We'd have to talk about what 'necessary' means."

I pleaded, "Does all of this have to come in tonight?"

"Maybe we should just watch the game on television right here," my father said, looking exhausted at the thought of moving more luggage.

"They will have bell captains at the hotel," my mother said reassuringly.

"Captains?" my father said incredulously. "They'll need platoons to get all this inside." Then he added gravely, "Let's make sure to stop at the ATM on the way out of town."

"We'll need a fortune for tips," I agreed. When I was growing up, my mother had so traumatized me about not tipping enough for any services that the first time I flew by myself, I tried to tip the stewardess. I was nine, I think.

When we finally got on the road to Nashville, my father announced, "If no one really needs me, I'm going to sleep," and promptly nodded off in the only part of the backseat that wasn't piled high with luggage.

It took only about ten minutes for me to remember what driving with my mother was like. I'm tempted to say it was a lot like *Driving Miss Daisy,* but it would be presumptuous to suggest I have Morgan Freeman's patience or charm. My mother approaches driving with the basic assumption that these annoying humans are on her road and she would prefer they disappear. Trucks, in particular, are taken as a personal affront. "Do they have to be so large?" she asked as a massive oil tanker passed us and a lumber truck in front swayed ominously. It was asked as if the size of the trucks reflected some personal overindulgence, like overweight families at the All You Can Eat dessert buffet lining up for fourths. A Ford pickup truck, looking small in comparison, honked at the oil truck, then swerved in front of us, accelerated, and quickly shot back into the passing lane.

My mother jolted backward and sighed loudly. To get her mind off the moment, I told her a story of driving in Italy on the Autostrada and being almost run off the road by tiny Fiats going a million miles an hour and then seeing one smash into a fuel truck, creating the most spectacular crash I'd ever seen. The satisfaction of it almost made up for the hours-long traffic jam that ensued. "Is this supposed to make me feel better?" she asked.

"Well . . ." She had a point. "This is a really big, safe car. We're fine."

She looked at me and smiled. "You can stop trying to make me feel better now."

"Is that because it won't work or you feel okay?"

"Good Lord," she murmured as two massive tractor trailers lumbered by, appearing to race each other to the next exit. I braked as one cut in front of us.

My father rose up from the backseat. "We're stopping?"

"No, I was just telling Mother about this crash in Italy when a little Fiat hit an oil tanker truck."

"Yeah? What happened?" my father asked eagerly.

"There was this explosion like—"

"Your son is trying to torture me," my mother interrupted.

"Why don't I drive?" Dad asked.

To my astonishment, the State of North Carolina had recently renewed his driver's license. He had to take a written and driving test, but he had passed. I felt like calling up the governor of North Carolina and asking, "Are you out of your mind? He's ninety-five!"

"I'm fine," I said. "It's not that far." My father took that as permission to fall back asleep while my mother tried to distract herself from thoughts of impending crashes by working on her epically long Christmas present list. I had grade school teachers who were still on that list.

It felt good to be driving to the first game of a new season. It was a time of limitless possibility, when every team was undefeated and the games stretched out tantalizingly, like a long buffet of favorite treats. All fans have different golden ages for their favorite sports, but I've observed it tends to be the time when your favorite team first finds great success. I was lucky. My love affair with Ole Miss football began when I was seven years old and Ole Miss won its first national championship.

My dad and I watched the games on a huge Zenith cabinet television in our basement. My mother never wanted a television in the living room. It had a remote control called Space Command that made funny sounds and vibrated like a tuning fork when you pressed the buttons. I played with it endlessly, discovering that if you hit it against something solid, it would send confusing signals that made the set dance through the few channels. This never failed to delight.

For the first six games of the 1959 season, Ole Miss allowed only one touchdown. They romped over everyone like gods playing mortals: Houston, Kentucky, Memphis State, Vanderbilt, Tulane.

Then came Arkansas, ranked number ten in the nation. My father would say, over and over, "The Hogs are tough, always tough." I'm not sure how old I was before I realized that hogs were animals as well as football players. The year before, Ole Miss had almost lost to them, barely squeaking out a two-point win in a brutal game. This year, Ole Miss was unstoppable, dominating the Hogs 28-0. Ole Miss's great fullback, Charlie Flowers, ran through Arkansas like a mule through corn. When Ole Miss scored, my dad would pick me up and swing me, and we'd yell together, "Go, Rebels!" It was probably then, swinging in my father's arms, that I began to fall in love with college football. How could I not?

After Arkansas came LSU. "LSU. LSU is always tough," he said.

"The Hogs were tough!" I shouted.

"But LSU . . ." His voice trailed off seriously. "LSU is special."

All that week, no one talked about anything but LSU versus Ole Miss. LSU ranked number one in the country. Ole Miss ranked number three. I was in the second grade at Power Elementary, and our teacher put a large Rebel flag on the wall. It was right next to the U.S. flag that we faced when we said the Pledge of Allegiance each morning. Naturally, I assumed we were pledging to both: the Ole Miss Rebels and the American flag. At seven years old, any connection to that thing called the Confederacy was totally lost. It was just the Ole Miss Rebel flag.

Today it would probably be called the Game of the Century. Maybe it was then, too; I don't remember. All that week, I fell asleep holding a Rebel flag. I had cut out the team roster from the *Jackson Daily News,* and every day I would go through it position by position.

When I got home from school on Friday, my father was at the house. This was unusual; he never got home much before supper. And he wasn't wearing a coat and tie. He was dressed like it was Saturday.

"What do you think about us going to see the Rebels play?"

I was confused. The Rebels played on Saturday. This was Friday. And then my mother was talking about what a long drive it was and we should be going, and then I slowly began to grasp it. But it still seemed impossible. We were going to see the Rebels play, and that meant not heading to the basement to watch them on the big cabinet television but in person. The Rebels versus the LSU Tigers. And LSU was tough.

It's a three-hour drive now from Jackson to Baton Rouge, but then it must have taken much longer. We stayed in a motel along the way, the first time I'd slept in a motel. The next day, the road seemed filled with cars with Rebel flags attached.

We parked what seemed like miles from the stadium. The streets were filled with swarming pirates with cutlasses, witches, and tigers. A lot of tigers. "It's Halloween," my father reminded me, pulling me a bit closer. In the distance, a giant structure loomed. Music and a strange roaring sound seemed to come from its depths. It was fascinating and terrifying. I stopped, wanting to go back to the car.

"It's okay," my father said, wiping my face, and then I realized I was crying. He pulled me up on his shoulders. "It's just football."

And so it was. And if this was football, how could anything else in life compete? The crowd was in a frenzy from the start. The Ole Miss section taunted the Tigers: "Hotty Toddy, God almighty! Who the hell are we? Flim Flam, Bim Bam, Ole Miss, by damn!" I'm sure I would have been terrified if my father hadn't pulled me tight and made me laugh.

Ole Miss kicked a field goal and played defense all night,

punting on second and third downs, daring LSU to score. All my favorite players were there—Charlie Flowers, the great quarterback Doug Elmore, Jake Gibbs.

Somehow I fell asleep and woke up to even more screaming and my father leaping to his feet, holding me. Down below Billy Cannon of LSU had fielded a punt from Jake Gibbs and was running through the entire Ole Miss team. Then there was only Gibbs between Cannon and the goal line. Cannon did something with his hips, and Gibbs grabbed at air, and Cannon trotted into the end zone. Seven to three, LSU over Ole Miss.

But the Rebels would come back; they always came back. "They'll get 'em," Dad said, and around us there was agreement.

They almost did. Ole Miss drove down the field. With seconds left on the clock, the quarterback Doug Elmore faked a handoff and rushed toward the goal, breaking a couple of tackles. But then Billy Cannon, playing defense as well as offense, as so many did in those days, hit him hard and with the cornerback Warren Rabb pushed him back.

It was over. LSU had won.

I had never seen grown-ups cry before, but they did that night, all around us, or so it seemed. I did too, of course. A lot, I think. Walking to the car, my father promised me the Rebels would come back and get another shot at LSU in the Sugar Bowl. I didn't know what the Sugar Bowl was, but I wanted to believe anything that was hopeful. Of course the Rebels would come back.

And on New Year's Day, a couple of months later, they did, just as my father promised. Ole Miss came back and beat LSU 21–0. The Rebels were named national champs in most postseason polls. National champions. As a boy in 1959, I knew there could be nothing so lucky in the entire world as to be from Mississippi and have the Rebels as your team.

A long line of cars was waiting to unload at the Marriott in Nashville. Most had Ole Miss logos of various sorts. Gone were the Rebel flags of old, replaced by a sweeping "Ole Miss" logo or the more understated "UM" given to the members of the booster club. My parents' Toyota had stickers from Groton, the Hill School, and Wellesley, the schools my sister's two daughters attended.

"We need to get some good Ole Miss stuff on this car," I said, impatiently waiting for the cars to creep forward. "Don't you think it's a little pretentious that we're driving to Ole Miss games with 'Wellesley' on the car?"

" 'Groton' is probably worse," my mother said, and I had to agree.

"I don't think anybody will be jealous of this car," Dad said, making a most reasonable point. Their Toyota was surrounded by fancy SUVs and the new sedans that all looked like Lexuses even if they weren't. Everyone seemed to be getting out and embracing each other like old friends at a bar, leaving their cars idling. I was remembering, not with great fondness, how much southerners liked to talk. No one was in a hurry. It would take forever to get inside the rooms.

I pulled out of the line and headed to self-park in a garage. "We can just walk from the parking garage," I said, relieved to be out of the line.

"How far is it?" my mother asked, and I glanced over at her worried expression. Of course, walking distance mattered to them, especially my father. It wasn't that he couldn't get around, but fifty yards versus a hundred yards mattered. It was the sort of stuff I wasn't used to thinking about, and it made me feel terrible.

"I can just let you out, and I'll go park," I said.

"Let's stay together," my dad said, and I glanced over at him and saw his concern. It suddenly hit me that the idea of being separated, of being in a confusing crowd, troubled him.

"The line is moving now," my mother suggested.

I turned the car around and lined back up for the Marriott drop-off. It was over ninety degrees outside, and I could see my father react when we finally got out of the car at the door. I grabbed a luggage cart, and a young bellman quickly followed. "Let me help with that," he said, then did a double take when I opened the trunk stuffed with luggage. "Maybe I should get two carts," he suggested gamely.

"We don't need all of this moved inside," I asserted, a bit wishfully. "At least, I don't think so." When I turned to seek my mother's help in luggage triage, I saw my father standing against a support for the entranceway. He didn't look great. He needed to get inside a nice air-conditioned room. "We just need a few things," she said to her young helper, who looked highly doubtful. I suspect he'd heard this before.

I left my mother to sort out the luggage and went inside the hotel. It was packed with Ole Miss fans, with check-in lines snaking around the lobby. Most seemed to know each other and had turned the registration into a tailgate party, drinks in hand. I spotted a thirtysomething fellow in a suit with a Marriott name tag who looked like a manager. "My dad's ninety-five and is waiting outside, and we really need to get him into a room, if that's possible?"

He looked immediately horrified. "It's awfully hot out there." He looked at me as if suspecting elder abuse. "Ninety-five?" he asked. I nodded. "I will deal with this," he said firmly, in the same voice airplane captains use to reassure passengers about severe turbulence. "Where's your father?"

I mumbled thanks and led him outside. In a few moments, he had my parents sitting on a lobby couch with large iced teas. Somewhere in the lobby, a voice rang out, "Are you ready?" It was met with a loud cheer, and perfectly reasonable-looking adults suddenly started chanting, "Hell yeah! Daaamn right! Hotty Toddy, God almighty! Who the hell are we? Flim Flam, Bim Bam, Ole Miss, by damn!"

Through the cheers and laughter, I looked over at my dad. He was holding up his iced tea in salute. The Marriott manager appeared holding room keys. He handed them over with an efficient smile. "Hotty Toddy," he said.

And using the proper call signal, I responded, "Hotty Toddy." Connection made. Over and out.

"There's really no reason to go to the game," my father announced.

I had to admit he had a point. The hotel was built right next to the Vanderbilt stadium, and the view from our room looked directly down onto the field. It was like nothing I'd ever seen or imagined existed. This room was the ultimate skybox. "This has to be better than our seats," he said.

"We've got great seats," I told him, which was true. "But . . ." I stared out the window onto the field.

"But they're there and we're here and here is good."

"That sounds profound," I admitted, which it did. "But they have hot dogs there, and we don't here."

He thought about it for a moment and jumped up on his feet. My dad is a big guy, and there were still moments when his natural athleticism unexpectedly surfaced. I was startled. "Let's go," he said.

The walk from the hotel to the stadium was no more than fifty yards. But as I was learning, these things took time. When I was in high school, I'd bought an old VW bus, and when I asked the guy who sold it to me how fast it would go, he thought about it for a moment and just said, "Son, I'd leave early." It was that way with my dad. Better to leave early.

We were swept along in a crowd of Vanderbilt students and Ole Miss fans, all headed for the stadium. I wasn't sure we were going to the right gate and told my father, "Wait here. I'll go check and come back." He was looking around and didn't seem to hear me. In front of us were the brilliant lights of the stadium. The Vanderbilt band was playing what I supposed was the Vandy fight song. People were laughing and hurrying to the game in the warm night air.

I thought back to those times when I had first been initiated to the wonders of football by my father. Then I had been the one walking slowly while he patiently waited for me. But some things hadn't changed. There was the stadium out there, glow-ing, the crowds, the expectation that anything could happen tonight and whatever did, we'd talk about it all week. He was still my father. I was still his son. And we still had this thing we loved to share.

"This is football," my dad finally said, smiling big. "Yes, sir, this is football." I smiled at him and took his elbow. "Are we sitting on the Ole Miss or Vandy side?" he asked.

"Vandy, I think. But I don't know which side is visitors or home."

He nodded at the gate in front of us. "This is home. Straight ahead."

"It is?" I pulled out the tickets to look for a gate number.

My father pointed. A stream of students poured into the gate. "Vandy side," he said again, and I realized he was right. The students were in black Vandy shirts, and there were a lot of them. It was like that with my father. There'd be these moments when I worried that he was confused, and then he'd say something that made it clear that he was more perceptive than I.

We were making our way to our seats—slowly—up the stadium ramp when a surprised voice rang out, "Phineas?"

Phineas is my father's first name. A jovial middle-aged man in Ole Miss garb put his arm around my dad.

"I can't believe you made it to the game!" he said.

"Well," my father said slowly, catching his breath a bit from the hike up the ramp, "I haven't yet."

"You look great! Rebels going to win tonight?"

"Beat 'em like a borrowed mule," my dad said.

"You got it!" The man laughed and moved on in a stream of fans.

"Who was that?" I asked.

My father thought for a second. "I have no idea."

You had to love Vanderbilt. Before the game, the entire freshman class ran out of the stadium tunnel through the goalposts onto the field, just like the real-deal football team that would follow in a few minutes. The stadium announcer boomed their names, and the giddy kids waved to the crowd like SEC champions. It was a hot night with a light breeze, and all around us fans had the happy, expectant sounds of the first game. I tried to remember how long it had been since my dad and I were sitting together in the stands, but I couldn't bring up the last time. I started to ask my father, but he slapped my thigh with one of his large hands, a gesture I remembered from our earliest days together at games, and said, "This is great. Just great."

And suddenly it didn't matter how long it had been, just that it was happening now.

The Rebels took the field led by Coach Hugh Freeze, a model for a new breed of coaches, the sort of anti–Bear Bryant. He smiled more than he scowled, hugged his players more than yelled at them, and generally seemed to give every impression that he considered himself the luckiest guy in the world. Born in Oxford, he had paid his dues as a high school coach and college assistant long enough to know he might never get a shot at the big time and wasn't the least bit coy that he had landed his dream job. When asked if he might be using Ole Miss as a stepping-stone to a bigger job, he flatly announced, "I hope to retire right here." Instead of scaring the players to death, Freeze's approach was to love 'em to death. "We are a family" was his mantra, "and because we love each other, we will never let each other down." If there had been a hint of mannered calculation to the sentiment, it might have tilted Freeze into the manipulative phoniness of a televangelist. But from him, it came across as a simple declaration of a worldview: this is who I am, this is how I feel and what I believe, and this is how we will win.

In his first year, without the benefit of a recruiting class he could call his own, Freeze turned a 2-10 record into 7-6 and took Ole Miss to a victory over the Pittsburgh Panthers in the Compass Bowl. That year, they lost heartbreakingly close games to LSU, Vanderbilt, and Texas A&M, coming within just a few plays of a miracle season. Freeze spent the postseason in a recruiting frenzy, bringing in one of the nation's top classes. His prize jewel was Robert Nkemdiche, a six-foot-five, 294-pound beast of a defensive player, considered by many the nation's number one high school talent. His older brother, Denzel, was already a sophomore star at Ole Miss. There were others. From Crete, Illinois, Freeze had snagged the best high school receiver in the country, Laquon Treadwell. He'd been selected the top high school athlete in Illinois and already had a nickname—SuccessfulQuon— and a Twitter account with thousands of followers. Nkemdiche and Treadwell were joined by other potential superstar freshmen: Cody Prewitt, a defensive back; Evan Engram, a huge tight end with world-class speed; a pair of offensive tackles, Laremy Tunsil and Austin Golson. Now these freshman stars were taking the field for the first time.

"Excuse me, but can I ask why you are wearing black?" The question came from an attractive woman in her thirties sitting next to my dad. "I heard you talking, and I know you are Rebel fans," she said with a smile. "And that black shirt, I'm sorry, but that just won't do."

My father looked over at me, nodding his head. He was wearing red, which was the designated Ole Miss color for the night. I was wearing a black polo shirt I'd thrown in my suitcase. It hadn't occurred to me when I put it on that black and gold were Vandy colors. I was surrounded by a sea of black shirts.

She held out her hand. "I'm Margaret Rawlings. I'm a Rebel, but my husband"—she nodded to the nice-looking guy next to her, deep in concentration studying the program as the starting lineups were announced—"he went to Vanderbilt. It's a mixed marriage, you know."

We introduced ourselves. "I didn't wear this because it was a Vandy shirt," I said, feeling suddenly very guilty. "I just didn't think about it." It seemed like a lame excuse, like trying to explain why you were leaving the grocery store with a couple of steaks stuffed under your coat.

"I knew it was a red night," my father said.

She laughed. "You are not helping him," she said.

"How'd you know?" I asked my dad.

"Your mother told me."

"Why didn't you tell me?" I asked.

"You're an age to dress yourself," he said, smiling. "And I never thought it mattered." He looked around and shrugged. "Guess I was wrong."

Our seatmate leaned in and said in a not so low voice, "This is always one of the worst nights of the year for me and my husband. Maybe this makes me a bad person or wife . . ." She nodded back at her husband. "But I hope he is goddamn miserable for the next couple of hours." Then she leaned back and yelled, "Go, Rebels!" I caught a whiff of bourbon and saw her husband pouring from a small flask into a Coke. That sweet smell on a warm night combined with the sounds of the game brought back a rush of memories. It was night. There was football. And there was drinking.

On the second pass of the night, one of the Ole Miss freshmen, Tony Conner, ripped the ball away from the Vanderbilt receiver for an interception. He was eighteen and on the fourth play of his first game in the toughest league in college sports and playing as if he owned the field. A couple of plays later and Ole Miss brought out its field goal kicker, Andrew Ritter. He was a fifth-year senior who had spent his career handling kickoffs. In his five years on the team, he'd never kicked a field goal. He had been scheduled to graduate the previous year, but Freeze had asked him to sit out a year, saving eligibility for the chance to return and compete for the job as the starting field goal kicker. It was a risk, but he had taken it and was now lining up for his first college kick. He made it easily.

It is this sense of possibility that helps make college sports so appealing. These days, professional athletes mostly appear to be of a different species: so big, so fast, so agile that, while they dazzle, they seem separated from us mere mortals. But here at Vanderbilt, there were young kids on both teams who had been in high school a few months earlier, and while they were all superb athletes—the SEC draws the best of the country—they retained an aura of normalcy that made you cheer for them all the louder. They were regular kids, just better, more dedicated.

It's not just that you wanted your team to win; you wanted the players to succeed.

Across the field in the Ole Miss student section, the inevitable cry went up, "Are you ready?" I watched my father smile as he followed along softly, "Hell yes. Hotty Toddy, God almighty! Who the hell are we? Flim Flam, Bim Bam, Ole Miss, by damn!" He looked out over the field, smiling, then repeated, with a silly grin, "By damn."

The first quarter was all Ole Miss, sharply executed plays, moving almost at will. But then it turned. Vanderbilt put together a solid if unspectacular drive to score, making it 10–7. After Ole Miss stalled, Vandy got the ball back and hit their best player, the wide receiver Jordan Matthews, with a short screen that he took fifty-five yards into the end zone. One play, fifty-five yards. Ole Miss 10, Vandy 14.

We were sitting in the first row, directly behind the Vanderbilt bench, where Matthews came running into his coach's arms. Vanderbilt's coach, James Franklin, was forty-one, the third African American head coach in SEC history. Charismatic, with high energy, he had brought Vanderbilt a new hope and interest in its football team. (At the end of the season, he'd leave Vandy for Penn State, taking top recruits with him and leaving massive ill will in his wake. But for now, he was the chosen one leading them to the promised land.) Matthews lifted Franklin up as if he were a kid. They were both laughing. I wanted Ole Miss to win in the worst way, but it was impossible not to enjoy the exuberance and sheer joy exploding a few feet away. It was like watching two loved ones meeting at an airport and jumping into each other's arms.

"He's quick," my father said, nodding at Matthews. At six feet three and 206 pounds, he was big, but it was his pure athletic grace that was so striking. He did a stutter-step dance, then leaped up for the classic chest bump with another player. It was ballet with a hint of violence.

A couple of minutes later, Vanderbilt scored again. Now Ole Miss was down 21–10, and the twenty-one unanswered points by Vandy made it feel much worse.

"I liked the first game better," Dad said. For a moment, I thought he was confused. But then I saw him smiling, and I got it. First game, as in this had been not only two quarters but two different games, one dominated by Ole Miss, one by Vandy.

As the teams jogged off at halftime, I asked my father how he was doing. It had occurred to me that he might only have the stamina or interest level for a single half, which would have been fine. It was stunningly hot. We could walk back across the street and watch the rest of the game from the hotel window. But he was completely transfixed, hanging on every play and feeding off the energy of the crowd. He flagged down a hot dog vendor, bringing out his ancient wallet, waving me off when I reached for my own. "On me," he said, and I think we both enjoyed a scene from our past: a good game, Dad buying hot dogs. We always got three, to share the extra. One each just never seemed enough.

"What do you think?" I asked as we watched the Vanderbilt band take the field. This was how we always did it, going back over the big moments of the first half over hot dogs while waiting for the second half to begin.

"I like the Ole Miss speed," Dad said. "The way they use so many receivers."

This launched us into a critique of the speedy spread offense. If you like football, you had to love the fast offense embraced by Hugh Freeze. He called it "basketball on grass" because it allowed players to improvise and maximize speed. It was basically an extension of the two-minute offense played over the entire game. Gone were traditional huddles; rarely did the quarterback take the snap directly from the center. Coaches signaled plays with giant cards waved by reserve players, making the sidelines resemble some mad gambling tournament. It was known as a "spread" for its pattern of putting players on the far right and left of the field, "spreading" the distance defenses must cover. Gone were the days of twenty-two players stacked up against one another in the middle of the field.

"It's got a lot of single wing in it," my father said. "A lot of fakes and deceptions."

"The single wing is coming back in some high schools. They do great with it. Nobody knows how to defend it."

He lit up at the thought. "I'd love to go see some of those games. We should find out where and go see them. Single wing was all we ever played."

We talked football until the second half started. It was one of those frustrating back-and-forths, with Ole Miss playing good football but Vanderbilt just a little better. Every time Ole Miss scored, Vanderbilt came back, and with just a minute to play, they led Ole Miss by three. "I can't believe we're losing to Vanderbilt," I said, sinking into a pre-defeat funk. "Vanderbilt? This is going to ruin the whole season. It's one thing to be 0-1, but 0-1 against Vandy?"

I looked over at our fellow Rebel fan with the Vandy husband. She looked even more depressed than I did. The prospect of a year spent with a gloating spouse must have been bleak.

"Field goal will tie it," Dad said. He was always optimistic. I admired that but didn't remotely share it. I was sure we were doomed. I was already working through my loss adjustment strategy. It's only a game. It's not bad.

Ole Miss was on their own eighteen-yard line and going nowhere. The quarterback Bo Wallace threw an incomplete pass. This is terrible, I was thinking.

Then, with the Vandy defense totally focused on stopping passes, Freeze called a running play straight up the middle. Jeff Scott, the compact, lightning-quick running back from Miami, shot through a break and was suddenly in a race for the end zone. In one of those wonderful moments in sports that you can't quite believe, Scott juked the last Vanderbilt defender and crossed into the end zone with a couple of seconds left on the clock. My father and I leaped to our feet, hugging each other, surrounded by stunned Vanderbilt fans. "I knew it!" Dad yelled. "I knew it!"

Ole Miss 39, Vanderbilt 35. Final.

It was one of those small miracles that make all the pains of fandom worthwhile. Dad and I stood there, my arm around his shoulders, his around mine, completely happy. A very tired-looking Vandy fan in his thirties—nothing is as exhausting as losing—shook his head and pulled his red-eyed son, maybe eight or nine years old, closer. "Y'all played a real good game," he graciously said.

"Got lucky there at the end," Dad said.

"I wouldn't say you didn't," the Vandy fan said and smiled that painful smile of defeat. They walked off, and I thought of how many times I'd walked away from games with my dad, looking to him to make the loss hurt less or the win last longer.

"It's hot," Dad announced. "Damn hot." I was losing my postgame adrenaline and starting to wilt. Across the field, the Ole Miss student section and band hadn't moved. The band had broken into a medley that included the shortened, politically correct version of "Dixie." It drifted across the field in the hot air and brought back a million memories of past games. Still, it seemed a bit rude to be flaunting victory so broadly in the backyard of these nice Vanderbilt folks, who were clearly hurting.

"We just kicked their goddamn ass," our female seatmate shouted. "Hotty Toddy." Her husband sat dejectedly, flask in hand. He seemed to have drunk himself into a very toasty stupor.

"Jeff Scott!" he suddenly announced, springing to his feet. "Son of a bitch, Jeff Scott! All they had to do was tackle one little guy! He's a leprechaun!"

That did make a certain amount of sense. Scott was only five feet seven and 170 pounds max.

He did a little jig with an angry face. "Why can't Vandy tackle a goddamn leprechaun?"

We all looked at him for a second, and then his wife started to laugh and that seemed to make him angrier for a second, and then he joined in and they walked off. At the end of the row, he did another jig.

"It was a good game," Dad said.

"It was a good game."

3

After Vanderbilt, Ole Miss returned to Oxford for their first home game. My parents and I drove down from Asheville. It was a long day, but after the last-minute win against Vandy, we were eager to get to the next game. Sports is funny that way. Had Ole Miss lost, the next game would have been tainted with fear of more pain. But even a last-minute victory against the traditionally weakest team in the SEC was enough to convince us that this was going to be a great season. The Rebels were playing Southeast Missouri State, a college none of us had heard of, which made it tempting to assume Ole Miss would win. But my father reminded me of a previous "certain" victory that had turned into a humiliating defeat.

"Jacksonville State," Dad said, "2010 and they beat us 49–48 in overtime."

"I remember," I said, sighing. "It was horrible. In overtime. How in God's name did Jacksonville State score forty-nine points?"

"How did Ole Miss score only forty-eight?" he asked.

"Can we talk about something more pleasant?" my mother asked from the backseat, where she had been reading. She was right. Thinking about a disastrous game like that could induce the sports version of post-traumatic stress.

For the weekend, we had rented a little house outside Oxford in a tiny community called Taylor. It was famous for a restaurant called Taylor Grocery, which had developed a cult following for its catfish. The game started at 6:00 p.m., which was an odd, happy-hour sort of kickoff time but perfect for Ole Miss. The partying in the Grove always began at least four hours before game time. For a 2:00 p.m. kickoff, that meant the drinking would begin around 10:00 in the morning, which wasn't a terrible thing, but it did take some combination of practice and natural ability. The problem with night games was that the pregame partying inevitably went on a little too long and a third-quarter hangover could become a serious problem. But for a 6:00 p.m. kickoff, you could sleep late, get something to eat in town, and still be drinking with family and friends at a perfectly respectable mid-afternoon hour.

On the morning of the game, my mother, who enjoyed football but had no desire to go to the games, announced she would hang out at the Kappa Kappa Gamma sorority house while Dad and I were at the game. This was the sorority that had brought her to Mississippi when she had come from LSU as a sophomore to "colonize" its first chapter at Ole Miss. She still had the combination of charm and iron will that had made the Kappa launch a great success.

I was headed out for a run but stopped in the door and turned around.

"You're joking, right?" I asked, sounding a little too hopeful.

My mother looked at me in surprise. "I'll drop you and your dad off and then just go over to the house."

"It's a great idea," my father chimed in.

I had to admit there was something about my eighty-six-year-old mother at the Kappa house during the game that was sort of wonderful. But it was obviously total lunacy.

"You're going to hang out with a bunch of drunk sorority girls?"

She made a face. "Don't be mean. They're Kappas."

"They probably won't get too drunk until after the game," my father said. "It's an early game."

"Pacing is important," I agreed.

My mother sighed. "I think I know more about Kappa girls than you do. When is the last time you were in a Kappa house?"

I wasn't about to argue. "Why don't you just stay here during the game? It'll be crazy on campus." She looked over at my dad in a way that said clearly, "Please explain this to your son."

"I don't think it's a great idea," he replied.

"How come?"

"We're out here in the country. Your mother shouldn't be here alone at night."

"Country? There's art galleries and Taylor Grocery out here. It's not like we're in the northwest frontier provinces of Pakistan. It's far more dangerous at the Kappa house," I insisted. "The first home game? Do you have any idea how hard they will be partying?"

"I'm sure they will have the best party," my mother said, adding pointedly, "the nicest party."

"They always do," Dad agreed.

I headed out in the hot midday sun for my run. By the time I got back from navigating the dangers of Taylor, past the boutique art galleries and Taylor Grocery, my parents had settled on my mother's staying at the house.

"It'll be fine here," she said and sounded a touch relieved. I realized that she hadn't wanted to go to campus; it was just Dad worried about her.

My father was already dressed in the red Ole Miss polo shirt we'd picked up the day before on campus. "You ready for football?" he asked. It was a refrain we had shared since I was a kid. This was before "Are you ready for some football?" became a popular riff in promo ads and game-day hype. When I was growing up, it was our own code, like a password to another special Saturday. "You ready for football?"

"Are they going to win?" I asked.

"Does it matter?"

It made us both smile. It always did.

"It's a good day for a game," Dad said. That was part of the ritual as well. It could be pouring rain or sleeting, and it would still be a good day for a game.

"Great day," I said, reciting my part.

For this season, the university had started new game-day parking regulations involving a complicated system of off-campus bus shuttles. The only way to get on campus was with a parking pass, which mostly went to season ticket holders and donors to various building and scholarship funds. But I'd been lucky enough to snag a pass through the kindness of the athletic department. My dad was the oldest living member of the Ole Miss Student Hall of Fame, and that he still wanted to come to games seemed to please the university a great deal.

We drove onto campus around 4:00 p.m. for the 6:00 p.m. kickoff. As we parked just off All-American Drive and were getting out of the car, I grabbed from the car a campus map that I'd picked up earlier at the Rebel Shop. That had been a mandatory stop to buy the matching Ole Miss shirts that we were wearing.

"What's that?" my father asked, sounding like a suspicious TSA agent eyeing a chain saw in your carry-on.

"It's a map." Then I added, as if it were necessary, "A campus map." Good to clear that up, in case he thought I was bringing, say, a map of Quebec.

He shook his head, looking pained. "The day I need a map to get around the Ole Miss campus . . ." He let it hang there, unfinished.

"Okay, but what about me? You know I haven't been here in years."

"Stick with me," he said gravely, as though we were heading out on a dangerous patrol.

As my dad and I slowly made our way across campus to the Grove, it was like walking into a huge reunion of a very extended family. If you didn't recognize someone immediately, the odds were still overwhelming that you would enjoy getting to know anyone you met, at least after a couple of drinks and some trash talk about the impending Rebel victory. It was the exact opposite experience of walking through Manhattan at rush hour. Yes, both were crowded, but here no one hesitated to make eye contact, smile, and greet one another with a nod and "Hotty Toddy." Of course, my initial reaction was to pull back, as though the next level of friendliness would invariably be intrusive and awkward and probably involve a request for money or at least football tickets. But by the time my father and I had reached the Circle by the Lyceum, it was all starting to feel perfectly normal. It was probably what visiting a nudist colony was like: a little odd at first but pleasant after a while, as long as it was warm.

And it was warm, too warm. I looked over at my dad and was startled that he was drenched in sweat and red-faced. My mother had stuck an inhaler and a little bottle of tiny nitroglycerin tablets in my pocket. I wondered if he might need one or both. A couple in their forties saw me looking at my dad with concern and stopped to ask, "Y'all doing okay?"

"Hotty Toddy," Dad said automatically, managing a smile.

"Hotty Toddy to you, good-looking," the woman said, taking his arm and looking over at me questioningly. I shrugged.

"It's hot," I said stupidly, not really knowing what else to say.

"Real hot," her husband agreed. "You know, we were just right inside there, and it's nice and air-conditioned. Might want to cool off in there." He motioned to a large building behind us: Brevard Hall.

"That sounds real good," Dad said but didn't move. He was looking out at the scene in the Circle with a smile. In front of us were hundreds of red party tents inside a half-mile circular drive. To our left was the Lyceum, the oldest building on campus, built in 1848 in imposing Greek Revival style, with half a dozen columns.

"You know," he said, "when I first came up to Ole Miss as a freshman, those columns weren't any more big around than this." He held out his hands about eighteen inches apart. The couple looked at him, then me, then saw the smile on his face, and we all started laughing.

"When was that?" the woman asked.

"Nineteen thirty-six," he said.

There was a pause as she did some math, then she asked, "How old are you?"

"Ninety-five," he answered. "Ninety-six in December."

"Good God almighty," the woman said, tightening her grip on his arm. "And you're going to the game?"

"Yes, ma'am. We went to the Vandy game, too," he said with a trace of pride. "That was a hell of a game."

The husband looked at his wife. "I told you we should have gone. I mean, he went and he's ninety-five!"

"When you're ninety-five, I promise you we'll go."

"When I'm ninety-five, you'll want to bring your boyfriend."

"I sure hope so." They were laughing.

I took my dad's arm, and she let her hand drop. "I think we should go inside and cool off," I said.

"You do that," she said, "then come on over to our tent," pointing across the Circle toward a tall statue at the bottom of the Circle; it was a memorial to Confederate soldiers. "We're over by the statue. Same place every year. Kind of a boring group, but we try."

My father waved, and we turned around to go inside Brevard Hall.

"This is the chemistry building," my father said as we stepped inside the cool brick building. "I think I had some classes in here."

There was a desk by the entrance with a campus security guard, a middle-aged African American woman who looked at us curiously.

"How you doing?" she asked. She looked hard at my father. "You okay?"

"Fine. This is the chemistry building, isn't it?" my father asked.

She looked at him in surprise and smiled. "It was. Old Chem, they called it."

"I'm old," my father said.

She laughed. "But now it's Brevard Hall. Chemistry moved."

"If chemistry moved out," my father asked, sitting down on a plastic chair near the guard's desk, "what moved in?"

"The National Center for Computational Hydroscience," I said, reading from a pamphlet I'd picked up by the entrance. "And the Mississippi Mineral Resources Institute. And a computer lab."

"I don't know what any of that is, but it sounds important," Dad said.

"Got a dean's office too," the guard said.

"Been to the dean's office a few times," my father said.

The security guard laughed and asked, "So what y'all doing now?" She looked at my father with a sweet concern.

"Cooling off," Dad answered.

"Ain't it the truth," she said, nodding. "You planning on going to the game in that long-sleeved shirt?"

I looked at my father, and it dawned on me that under his Ole Miss polo shirt he was wearing a long-sleeved shirt.

"What are you doing in that thing?" I asked.

"Your mother thought I should wear it."

For some reason, I hadn't noticed.

"There's a bathroom over there. You can take it off. Or do it right here. I don't mind." She laughed.

The bathroom was stone and marble with a slight echo. I doused my face in cold water and, when I came up, saw my father struggling to get his Ole Miss polo shirt off. "This damn thing," he muttered as I turned to help him ease the shirt off. I thought of the countless times he'd helped me dress or undress, how he'd taught me how to knot ties in half a dozen different ways and shown me how to put on football shoulder pads. Now it was my turn to help, wishing I could slip time backward so there was no need. He had run marathons into his seventies, rarely been sick. But now he was ninety-five.

We carefully peeled off the polo shirt and the long-sleeved shirt underneath it. It was a button-down blue oxford dress shirt, soaking wet. I helped him unbutton it and rolled it up. "I'll carry this." He nodded, then started to put his Ole Miss shirt back on. Even at ninety-five, he was still strong, which only meant he had once been very strong. He got it back on, dug a comb out of his back pocket, and worked on his hair. For some reason, it was longer than I remembered, mostly a whitish gray but not completely.

"I look terrible," he said with a smile. His eyes caught mine in the mirror. We both laughed and walked out.

"You come on back if you need to cool off," the security guard said. "Go, Rebels."

Since we had been inside, the crowd in the Circle had grown. Various friends had told me where they had tents before the game, and I'd promised to drop by, thinking it would be easy to find them. But this was like a color-coordinated—red—refugee camp for what seemed like half the football fans in America. "Let's go over to the flagpole," Dad said, pointing to the center of the Circle.

It was hard to believe this was exactly where a pitched battle had been fought on September 30, 1962, the day James Mer-

edith was brought to Ole Miss by federal marshals for enroll-
ment. In the Civil War, the Lyceum had served as a Confederate
hospital, and on the night of the Meredith riot it was once again
transformed into a combat aid station. In *The Race Beat,* their
great book on civil-rights-era reporting, Gene Roberts and Hank
Klibanoff describe a terrible scene inside the Lyceum that night:
"Bloodstains on the floor. Bandaged marshals lying exhausted
on the floor . . . A marshal from Indianapolis had gotten shot in
the throat; blood spurted with the rhythm of his beating heart
and his condition deteriorated as he lost blood."

Two men died that night, a Mississippian in his twenties and
a French journalist. In accounts, the young Mississippian seems
invariably referred to as a "jukebox repairman," as if the sheer
ordinary and casual charm of his profession made his death
more absurd. He was struck in the forehead, most likely by a
stray shot. The journalist was shot in the back and the head,
probably targeted intentionally as many newsmen were that
night.

In the 1968 Chicago riots at the Democratic National Convention, protesters famously chanted, "The whole world's watching,"
as both a taunt to the police and a validation of the importance
of their actions. But that night in Oxford, first in the soft dusk of
a hot Mississippi evening and then in the darkness that seemed
to last too long, the rioters didn't want the world to watch; they
wanted the world to go away.

It was both the first student riot of the 1960s and the last
battle of the Civil War. It was here, in front of the Lyceum, that
the University Greys had mustered in 1861 to fight the Federals;
all but three students joined up. In Pickett's Charge at Gettys-

burg, every Grey was killed, wounded, or captured. One hundred years later, armed Federals had returned, and there was no desire to lose again.

That Saturday night in 1962, when my father and I got home early from the stadium where Ole Miss was grinding out a win over Kentucky, the game was still in the fourth quarter. My mother was listening on the radio. "That son of a bitch," she said, meaning Ross Barnett. "That little son of a bitch." She and my father disappeared back into their bedroom, and I went into the kitchen. Elzoria was there, putting away food after the party. She was listening to the gospel music she loved, but I talked her into changing stations so I could hear the last of the game. I helped her bring in glasses while the game played out to its finish. I cheered every Rebel first down.

Elzoria Kent had worked for my family all my life. It would be that southern cliché of a certain era to say she raised me, but of course that was true. She was short and athletic, with a quick wit and laugh and an ability to find that touch of the absurd that never seemed to lurk far from the surface in the strangely textured world of the South. We could and did laugh about just about anything. I can't ever remember there being anything I wouldn't talk to her about; she was more an older best friend than a parent, and I asked her advice on everything.

"I heard Mr. Barnett speak," she said. She always referred to him as "Mr. Barnett."

"We left at the half. Daddy wanted to go," I said. "Ole Miss is going to beat everybody this year. Just you watch. Everybody."

"Well, wouldn't that be something," she said, smiling. She held up a plate of cobbler. "You don't want some of this by and by, do you?"

I sat and finished the cobbler while listening to the Rebels win, 14–0.

"You know something about your mama?" Elzoria said, bringing in some serving plates that had leftover baked ham and sweet potatoes. "She is a handsome waster," she said, then chuckled. "I love Mrs. Stevens to death, but she is one handsome waster."

"The Rebels are the best team in the whole world," I said to her.

"Isn't that something," she said, poking me lightly with a fork. I laughed. She always made me laugh. Then she sat down to eat ham, and we had some of her cobbler together and listened to the postgame show.

The next night, President Kennedy addressed the nation on the integration of Ole Miss. He spoke while the riots were erupting but astoundingly was unaware of the violence. "Mr. James Meredith is now in residence on the campus of the University of Mississippi. This has been accomplished thus far without the use of National Guard or other troops."

"Thank God," my mother said.

We were all watching together, my sister and my mother and father. Like the president, we had no idea of what was happening in Oxford. I was wearing pj's that had cowboys and Indians on them. For some reason, my mother saved the top of these, and I found it years later, stuffed in a box at our house down on the Mississippi Gulf Coast. It was moldy with salt air, and for a moment I stared at it, thinking it was an old rag that had been used to wrap pictures. But then I saw the cowboys with the big hats and the lassos, and it came rushing back to me.

I stood up to go to my room. My mother motioned for me

to sit back down to watch. The whole thing was confusing. I didn't understand about integration or James Meredith or why the president was mad at us. "Why does everybody hate us anyway? What did we do?"

My father pulled me into his lap. "Nobody hates us. Some people just do bad things. That's all."

That night, Dad came and sat on my bed, and we talked about what a great team the Rebels had and how they could win another national championship. "They won't take that away, will they," I asked, "just because the president is mad at us?"

He told me the president wasn't mad and he was a good man. "Some people are full of hate for things they don't understand. But there are more good people than bad people." He nodded to the Ole Miss roster I had taped by my bed. "The Rebels are good this year. Real good."

That made me feel better. If the Rebels were good, everything would work out.

At school the next day after lunch, our teacher, Mrs. Davis, came in red-eyed. We liked her a lot, and it was clear she was upset. She told us the headmaster wanted to talk to us.

In the third grade, I had transferred from the public school in our neighborhood to a tiny Episcopal elementary school, St. Andrew's. Later, because of the work of my mother and others who followed her, it would grow into probably the state's best school, with grades one through twelve and a campus like a small college on the outskirts of Jackson. But when I was there, it was just a handful of what seemed to be oddball students in a once grand mansion near collapse that had been donated as some sort of tax write-off. Much of Jackson had been burned when Sherman came through during the Civil War, but this house had been spared, most likely used as housing for Union officers.

The headmaster, the Reverend Marshall James, was a bubbly sort of clergyman, impossible not to like. He was one of those irrepressibly visionary types who could turn the frequently blown fuses of the old house's ancient wiring into a science lesson. He always smiled and laughed at the worst jokes, but today he came into our classroom looking very somber. While Mrs. Davis stood off to the side, the headmaster faced us, his hands behind his back.

"Ladies and gentlemen"—he always called us this—"this weekend a terrible tragedy occurred at the University of Mississippi." I can remember thinking that something horrible must have happened to the Rebel team. "Two innocent souls were lost in needless violence." He stopped, and then I realized that he was trying not to tear up. "A single American Negro named James Meredith was admitted to the University of Mississippi. This was in accordance with the laws of this great nation and state. The president spoke of this last night on national television."

There was rustling in the classroom now. Meredith and Kennedy were subjects people talked about, and a lot of the kids around me had parents who weren't happy with either of them.

"There was much violence on the campus. You will hear a lot about this in the days and weeks ahead. We will discuss this here at school. But I always want you to remember that it is our duty, as servants of the Lord, to view the world with love in our hearts, not anger or hate. We must drive out hate with love. God loves each and every one of his creations, and God made us all in his image. We know that, because the Bible tells us so."

This was a refrain from a song we often sang in school and in Sunday school:

Jesus loves me! This I know,
For the Bible tells me so;
Little ones to Him belong;
They are weak, but He is strong.

Refrain:

Yes, Jesus loves me!
Yes, Jesus loves me!
Yes, Jesus loves me!
The Bible tells me so.

A lot of students were crying now. I can't remember if I was. Probably.

"This is a sad day for Mississippi and America," he said. "But we will have brighter days. I want you to always remember that, ladies and gentlemen, we will have brighter days, and it is your responsibility to bring more light into this world. And I know each of you will. Now let us pray. Our Father who art in Heaven . . ."

After the riot on Sunday, September 30, 1962, Ole Miss was scheduled to play Houston in its homecoming game in Oxford the following Saturday. Coach Johnny Vaught describes the

scene in his book, *Rebel Coach:* "It looked to me like 5,000 can-
isters of tear gas had been used. The campus resembled a trash
dump. By midweek, helicopters were landing on our practice
fields. Each day when we worked out there were a couple of
thousand troops standing around watching us."

No one knew where Saturday's game should be played, and
some wanted it canceled. This was a matter of discussion at the
highest levels of the U.S. government. Attorney General Robert
Kennedy called Coach Vaught to discuss. Assistant Attorney
General Nicholas Katzenbach (later AG under President Johnson) met with Coach Vaught several times. On Wednesday,
the Memphis *Commercial Appeal* ran a story confirming that
the homecoming would continue as planned in Oxford: "The
University reconfirmed its decision to carry on normal Homecoming activities at Ole Miss, including the game with the University of Houston after more conferences with military and
Justice Department officials. United States Assistant Attorney
General Nicholas Katzenbach told a news conference: 'Meredith
has plans which will take him off the campus, irrespective of
whether the game is played or not.'"

As I walked through the Grove on a warm afternoon fifty-one
years later, it was hard to imagine an assistant attorney general
commenting on the game-day plans of one student at the University of Mississippi. But in retrospect, it seemed like a very
smart play to defuse any chance for those hoping to confront
Meredith on campus.

On Thursday, news accounts reported the game was being
moved to Houston, though that was never confirmed. Finally,
on Friday, Ole Miss announced that Jackson was the choice. It

was a homecoming that wasn't at home, but it made sense. This got the game out of Oxford but was still close enough for students to attend, heading off possible anger over the moving of the game to another state. Students and Ole Miss fans could come to the game, wave Confederate flags, yell for their team, and vent any frustrations. The high-level negotiations over the game reflected an appreciation for the power of the sport, at least among white Mississippians. It was an all-white team, and it seems a safe assumption that the fan base was mostly white. It would be fascinating to have some inkling of what black Mississippians thought of the Ole Miss Rebels in those days. Did they take pride that a university from their home state was a football power? Did they listen to Ole Miss defeat every team in that troubled year of 1962 and cheer? Did the team's being segregated mean support was segregated? None of my friends got excited when Jackson State had a great team, as they often did. We—black and white Mississippians—loved the same game but existed in our separate worlds. It would take years for football to start bringing races together in Mississippi.

But I wasn't thinking about that when I was nine years old and one of those white Mississippians; all I thought about was the Rebels winning another game and the chance to see my heroes in person. I remember when it was announced that Ole Miss would play in Jackson. It was on Friday morning, and I was in a gym class at St. Andrew's School. Because it was in an old house, St. Andrew's didn't really have a gym. We played basketball on cracked asphalt in back of the house under rims without nets and threw a football around on a stony dirt patch. My friend Stuart Irby told me about the game location. Later his life would come to a tragic end, but in our school-yard days, Stuart appeared sophisticated and worldly beyond his years. It seemed natural that he would know everything.

I went straight to the headmaster's office and asked to use the phone. His secretary, a kind woman who sang in the choir at St. Andrew's Church, came around from her desk and sat next to me in the cheap chairs that were for visitors. She asked me whom I wanted to call.

"I need to call my dad," I said. "It's important."

She nodded sweetly. "Is everything okay? Do you feel okay?"

"Didn't you hear?" I pleaded. "The Rebels are going to play tomorrow!"

It was a sign of St. Andrew's School's general benevolence that they actually let me call my dad. I reached him through his secretary. He had an office not too far away in Jackson's ugliest office building, called the Petroleum Building. It was a failed attempt at modern, covered with bright multicolored panels. My father always said the best thing about having an office in it was that you didn't have to look at it. I loved to visit him at his office and would play with spools of Dictaphone tape, a magical device that somehow captured his voice. He came on the phone, concerned. But I blurted out, "The Rebels are playing in Jackson on Saturday. Can we go?"

"I'd heard rumors about that," he said in a teasing voice. He was probably relieved that was all I was calling about. "Let's talk about it tonight," he said. "Everything okay at school?"

When I got in the car after school, I told my mother about the game and how I had called Dad. "It could be dangerous," she said. "Who knows what people might get up to after what just happened?" She said the same thing that night when we talked about it over dinner. My parents never argued at the dinner table, but this came close.

"It's a football game," my father said.

"It's the Rebels," I said. Who didn't want to go see the Rebels?

"You don't know what will happen," my mother insisted.

"They'll win," I said. "The Rebels always win."

"I want to go horseback riding," my sister, Susan, said. She had discovered horses and loved to go to Stockett Stables and ride. It was a place run by our cousin Robert Stockett, where you could rent horses. Robert was a kind, gruff man who told great stories and loved hanging out on the falling-down porch of his stable. Later Robert's granddaughter Kathryn would write about Jackson in *The Help*. My sister and I both enjoyed horses, like most kids, but Susan had started to develop a deep lifelong love of horses and riding. I just liked the trail rides and a chance to feel like a cowboy.

"We have to go see the Rebels," I pleaded.

But we didn't. The next morning, my dad told me we weren't going but that we'd go to other games. We were in the kitchen, and Elzoria was there. My dad made waffles. That was his thing on weekends. He loved to make them on a big hunk of waffle iron. I still have that thing, and it still works, though it looks like a part to a Russian tank that had gone through a long war. Every Saturday, he mixed up the batter and carefully poured it out, like casting gold ingots. When he closed the top, some of the batter always leaked. That was the best part. That batter on the outside would burn crisp, and I'd break it off while the waffle was still cooking, always managing to burn my fingers and my tongue.

"Mr. Stevens," Elzoria said, and my father nodded, carefully watching the waffle iron. "What's wrong with this world when you have to worry about going to a football game?"

My father turned and shook his head and looked as sad as I could remember. "Some people are just crazy."

She nodded. "Ain't that the truth?"

The waffle iron started to smoke. I yelled, and my dad turned back to lift the lid. This was always a big moment: to see what color the waffles had turned out.

"Crazy, crazy," my father said, carefully starting to lift the waffle. "And crazy mean."

Elzoria brought over a plate, and Dad placed the perfect waffle on it and started to pour another.

"Mr. Stevens," she asked, "why you reckon they don't want that boy to go to school?"

My father watched the batter spread out on the spikes of the iron. "I think they're scared, Elzoria," he said.

"Scared of one boy?" Elzoria scoffed.

"Scared he's smarter than they are and a whole lot of others are too."

"Can I tell you one thing, Mr. Stevens?"

"You can tell me anything in the world, and I wish you would."

Elzoria laughed. She opened up a metal tin of sugarcane molasses that we'd buy when we went out to the country. I scooped it out and watched it drip down on the waffle, like amber lava.

"I think if that's why they're scared, they probably right." And she laughed, covering her mouth. She was so tiny that when she laughed, she seemed to move up and down. "Once these boys and girls start going to college, there's not any stopping 'em. Least that's how I see it."

"Ain't that the truth," my father said, using one of Elzoria's favorite sayings.

Ole Miss crushed Houston 40–7 that afternoon. Houston had been undefeated, but it was as if the entire frustration and anger and humiliation and shame of the riots were unleashed on them. I walked down our street, Piedmont Street, to the end and could hear the crowd in the distance. I knew I shouldn't do it, but I kept walking toward the stadium. By Bailey Junior High School, I could see the stadium and hear the announcer, though I couldn't understand a word he said. I stayed there as long as I dared and then started to walk back home. On the way home, a car passed me with Rebel flags and I waved and they waved and a crew-cut driver yelled, "Go, Rebels!" and I yelled right back. That's what we Rebels did.

Ole Miss won the eight remaining games that season, outscoring opponents by 247 to 53 for the season. It was that magical season of every fan's dreams. Eventually, everybody quit talking about James Meredith and started talking about Fidel Castro and the Cuban missile crisis. I put extra batteries for my transistor radio in the crude fallout shelter my dad outfitted under the basement steps so that I would be sure not to miss any Rebel games if we moved in. It never occurred to me that if we were living under the stairs after a nuclear strike, the Rebels probably wouldn't be playing.

Almost fifty-one years later, the Grove was again filled but with tents and fans, not troops and rioters. My father and I took a while to work our way through the game-day crowd to the flag-pole at the center of the Circle. "Let's sit awhile," he said, edging down on the concrete base of the flagpole. It was crowded, and I'm certain that we were the only adults not drinking something strong.

The Lyceum was directly in front of us and the statue commemorating the Confederate war dead directly behind us at the base of the Circle. In the late afternoon and dusk of September 30, 1962, it had been mostly students here in the Circle. But as it grew dark, outsiders from across the state and beyond had joined them. In his wonderful memoir, *Dixie,* Curtis Wilkie, who was an Ole Miss student at the scene, writes, "Within a half hour of the outbreak of fighting, the state troopers—who had maintained roadblocks at the gates of the school to keep troublemakers away—withdrew, leaving the campus open to posses of night riders."

As the riot escalated, one of my childhood heroes, the legendarily tough linebacker and fullback Buck Randall, saw the bloodied bodies inside the Lyceum and went out on the steps and appealed for calm. But the riot had passed the point of being calmed by words, the madness of the moment bigger than even the toughest guy on the toughest team.

We walked down the center of the Circle toward the Confederate monument, surrounded by party tents with long tables overflowing with everything from ribs to casseroles. My dad spotted a particularly tasty collection of barbeque and moved toward it.

"We don't know these people," I whispered frantically. "We can't just walk up and take their food."

"Sure we can. Everybody does that."

"I don't think so."

"Phineas? Good God!" We looked up to see a smiling man elegantly dressed in a blazer and slacks. He had a bright white handkerchief artfully folded in his breast pocket. He was younger than my dad but not by much. They shook hands, and my dad took him by the forearm, the way he did when he was truly glad to see someone. The man turned to me and held out his hand, "Bill Threadgill. Your dad and I were in law school together."

"I was ahead of him in law school," Dad said. "I'm much, much older. What are you, Bill?"

He sighed. "Ninety. I know, you're older. Don't be showing off. You know what I did, Phinny? I bought a condo up here last year. Yes, sir, bought me a place here to come up for games and concerts. Just great."

His son, Tim, pulled us over to his tent. He was in his late forties, thin and athletic. He was a lawyer in my father's old firm, and I'd met him before at an event the law firm had for my dad's ninety-fifth birthday and we'd talked bicycles. He and a few friends had ridden the length of the Blue Ridge Parkway a couple of years before, passing through Asheville. My folks had come out on the parkway and met them for cheerleading and provisions. It was a trip I'd always wanted to make.

"We're all from Columbus," Tim gestured to his tent crowd, introducing us around. "Half these guys I went to high school with. We've been doing this for about ten years now." They had a long table filled with all sorts of food, folding chairs, and a huge television.

My father and I dug in to jambalaya. "How do you do all this?" Dad asked, nodding to the food spread, the tent, the chairs, the television. "It must be a lot of work."

Tim looked a bit sheepish. "Actually, we used to do it more

ourselves, but now there are these outfits that will just handle everything."

His wife laughed. "Except the food and the drinks. We still do that. But some folks, they go the whole catering route." She gestured over to a nearby tent. It was laid out with china and silver utensils and had a candelabra hanging down. Under it was a little sign that read DON'T WORRY, THIS IS NICER THAN OUR HOUSE. It was easy to see why many fans just stayed in the Grove and watched the games on television. The food was better than any at the stadium and the chairs as comfortable as you provided.

But Dad was eager to get to the game. "It's been years since we've been in the stadium," he said, putting his arm around me, and I realized I was excited in a way I hadn't been at the first game in Nashville. That had been a football game and a good one, but this was more: the first home game of the season and a stadium full of Rebel fans.

"I'm really glad we did this," I said to him.

"Me too," he said. "You know, I feel pretty good. I wasn't sure I was up for this but I feel pretty good." We thanked our impromptu hosts and started walking toward the stadium. As we passed the statue of the Confederate soldier, Dad said, "It was said in my day that the good soldier tips his hat to every virgin coed."

I laughed. We'd walk a little, then stop and rest, then walk a little more. From inside the stadium, we could hear the pregame videos that have become a staple of college football played on the scoreboard screen. Every couple of minutes, a raucous "Hotty Toddy" broke out.

"Do you remember when we would walk to Memorial Stadium from Bailey Junior High?" I asked as we rested on a stone wall near the stadium gate.

"Of course," he said. "Those were great games." He wiped off sweat with a handkerchief; he always carried a handkerchief. I don't think I'd had one since debutante dances. In front of us, a long line of fans streamed into the game. Several people recognized my father and called out. He'd wave and smile. "I remember how excited you would get at the games," he said. "You talked about them all week."

"I think I did all summer." We both laughed.

"It was when I really fell in love with football, walking to those games with you. I can remember almost running to keep up with you."

"Not a problem now," he said. "I'm moving slow. But we're almost there."

We could hear the stadium announcer introducing the Rebels' starting offense. It was time to go find our seats, but we both seemed content to wait.

"I wish we had gone to more games," I said.

"When?"

I shrugged. "The last twenty or thirty years."

He nodded. "That would have been nice, but you were busy, and we did other things."

"I shouldn't have been so busy. I don't know why I didn't make more time."

"It's what happens," he said. "I wish I hadn't worked as much as I did when you and your sister were growing up."

"Really?" I turned to him. We'd never talked about this sort of thing. "I know there are kids who think their dads weren't around enough, but I never felt that with you. Never."

"Good." He smiled, and I could see his eyes drift back to a different time. "But I missed too much. I spent a lot of nights in hotels when you were growing up. We had to go where the work was. We were still trying to get really established."

His law firm had grown from five members to the largest in Mississippi and one of the largest in the South. "It was an incredible achievement to turn it into what it is today," I said.

"It wasn't just me," he said, and that was always how he handled any praise about the firm.

"You know how you used to say, 'There is no limit to what can be achieved as long as no one cares who gets the credit'?" I asked.

"I still say that. Don't have to put it in past tense."

"Right." I felt scolded, as if I'd considered his expiration date had passed. "Do you remember where you heard that first?"

"You don't think I made it up?" he teased. "It was here at Ole Miss. A law school professor. Always stuck with me. Thought about it a lot when I was in the Navy."

The stadium behind us roared with the opening kickoff. We both got to our feet. "We have to get inside," he said. "They may need us."

We started moving toward the ticket gate. The crowd was almost gone, everyone inside cheering the Rebels.

"You know," I said, putting my arm around him and squeezing his shoulder, the way he used to do to me on our way to games, "I thought you were the best dad in the world. I still do."

He reached around and put his arm over my shoulders, so we were walking like two drunks.

"You're a great son. We've been lucky."

And when he said that, walking into the game, I felt like the luckiest man alive.

———

Our seats were in the first row, behind the Ole Miss bench. I'd bought them online, more for their ease of access than game-side appeal. The idea of hiking up many flights of stadium steps with my dad had seemed crazy, and that was even before I realized just how slowly he moved.

Like almost every major college football stadium, Ole Miss's had undergone a series of renovations, expanding its seating to just over 63,000. The latest work had been completed the past August, and although I had good memories of the old stadium, I had to say the changes had been done well. It didn't have the beautiful retro quality of the new baseball stadiums like Baltimore's Camden Yards and Nationals Park in Washington, D.C., but it seemed as though it belonged. You could still close your eyes and imagine Archie Manning running from LSU's future Hall of Famer Ronnie Estay, fake pumping to freeze the secondary, and then throwing across his body in his strange but deadly style.

"Hey, these are great seats," the man next to me said. He was wearing an Ole Miss shirt, and next to him was his young son, about ten, and college-aged daughter. She had her arm around her younger brother.

"Great seats," I agreed. We introduced ourselves, the sort of open camaraderie that came so naturally at a game with the assumption of shared interests. I nodded to his game program. "They say in there where Southeast Missouri State is?" I asked the man. "I don't think I've ever heard of them."

"Cape Girardeau, Missouri," he said without hesitation. "We live there, actually. It's my school."

I smiled the way you might if you walked into the wrong-sex bathroom by mistake. Smile. See, just a mistake, I'm not a bad guy. Honest.

"Really?" I asked. There was a chance he was just kidding me. There had to be. "But what are you . . ."

"My daughter's a freshman at Ole Miss. We came down for the game."

"That's fantastic," I said, overcompensating with way too much good cheer. "She liking it?"

"Loves it. You saw the scene today at the Grove. And she's a big lit major. We came down here and went to Faulkner's house."

"Rowan Oak," I said.

"Nothing like that at home." Then he nodded toward the Southeast Missouri players taking the field. "Don't worry. I know we're going to get killed."

He was right. By the end of the first quarter, Ole Miss was ahead 17–0. By the end of the second half, it was 31–0. The Rebels scored on five consecutive series, with two long passes of sixty-plus yards.

It was great fun. With games like this, at least for a while, it's easy to forget that the other team was way overmatched and start believing such easy success could be had against an SEC team. The sun dipped below the stadium, bringing a hint of coolness and a tease of the season changing. We ate a couple of hot dogs and listened to the Ole Miss coaches yell at their players. A team could be up by one hundred points, and coaches would still yell. Not angry, but excited, bringing order, keeping the players' minds in the game.

At the half, as the Ole Miss band started to move out on the field, we stood and stretched, feeling good about the world.

"You know," my dad said, "I bet they could win this second half without us."

"Do we risk it?" I asked. This was another ritual of ours if considering leaving a game when the Rebels were ahead. Do we think they could win it without us? Do we risk it? We once left a game when Ole Miss had what seemed an insurmountable lead, only to have them lose by the time we got back home. It was agony. There was no way not to believe that if we had stayed, it would have made the difference. I once explained this to my mother, and she countered, "That's why I don't sleep on planes. Who's going to fly the thing?"

We made our way out of the stadium into the falling light. I stood there, thinking. "I have no idea where we parked," I finally confessed.

My father looked at me and smiled. "That's what happens when you get to your age," he said, then led us directly to the car.

4

""

After Southeast Missouri, Ole Miss played the University of
Texas in Austin. We debated going to the game; my dad had
spent some time at Texas studying oil and gas law many years
ago, and I'd lived there for a year and a half during George W.
Bush's first campaign. We both had good memories of the place,
and when I reread the great Billy Lee Brammer's *Gay Place,* which
I tried to do every year, it always made me want to be back in the
Austin of clubs and beer gardens that he so beautifully describes.
Brammer wrote of the crowd around Lyndon Johnson, but forty
years later, when I was in Austin, the mix of political operatives,
lobbyists, students, press, and musicians felt seductively similar.

But in the end, my parents decided it was too far to drive, and
though we didn't admit it, we felt it was likely Ole Miss would
lose. The year before, Texas had trounced the Rebels 66-31 at
home in Oxford. This year, they were playing in the massive UT
stadium in front of a rabid Longhorn crowd, and it didn't seem
likely they would get out of Austin with a win. But to our astonished delight, Ole Miss dominated Texas, winning 44-23. That
made Ole Miss 3-0 and ranked in the top twenty teams in the
nation. The next game was against Alabama in Tuscaloosa, and
in the closing minutes of the Texas game the heady Ole Miss
fans chanted, "Bring on 'Bama."

My parents were back in Asheville, and I was in Los Angeles working on a television show, but we talked all through the game, calling each other after every Ole Miss score, astonished the Rebels were headed to an easy win. "This is the year!" I yelled over the phone to my dad. "This is it."

"Well," he said, "I imagine Alabama is thinking the same thing."

On the plane from L.A. to Atlanta, where I was going to meet my parents, I wore one of my growing collection of Ole Miss shirts and was amazed when several people on the plane saw the shirt and offered up "Hotty Toddy" or "Go to hell, Alabama." It made me feel like a member of some not-so-secret society, though I had to wonder if the team were 0–3 instead of 3–0, if the response would have been the same.

We spent the Friday night before the game in Atlanta and got an early start for the night game in Tuscaloosa. It was a beautiful, clear day, and the road was crowded with 'Bama faithful headed to the game. Every other car seemed to have a ROLL TIDE bumper sticker or Crimson Tide flag stuck to the windows.

Halfway to Tuscaloosa, we stopped in one of the many gas station-grocery store combinations that sold fried chicken and barbeque. Above the counter was a large sign: AT ALABAMA, WE DON'T REBUILD, WE RELOAD! My father nudged me, nodding to the sign. Then he said to the woman behind the counter, "We're Auburn fans."

She was punching out a complicated request for a lottery ticket and didn't look up. "Honey, the good Lord blesses all sinners."

My father laughed. "That he does."

She looked up and smiled. It was a worn smile of someone who had worked too many hours for too long for too little but had never really expected anything else. It wasn't bitter, just tired. "And if you want to be for those piss-poor-toilet-paper-throwing-sons-of-bitches, that's your own cross to bear."

A man behind us laughed and said, "This is 'Bama territory in here. My wife is a War Eagle, and she is scared to come in."

"Bobby," the woman said, "you know that's not right. We wouldn't hurt her."

"I've told her that."

"Just scare the crap out of her."

This broke everybody up.

"You're not worried that we're going to poison you like we poisoned those trees at Auburn?"

A younger woman behind the counter carrying an armful of cigarette cartons groaned. "That was awful. That man was two beers shy of a six-pack. Don't think that was about loving 'Bama. 'Bama fans hated that."

"We're really Ole Miss fans," my mother said. She'd been searching the store for something healthy to eat and finally settled on peanut butter crackers. It seemed least likely to kill you quickly.

"I was kidding about Auburn," Dad explained.

"Honey, we don't joke about that sort of thing," the woman said flatly. She didn't smile. "This ain't casual like Ole Miss and Miss State."

"I wouldn't call that casual," my mother said, laughing.

"I would, sweetie," the woman said, staring coolly at my mother.

Outside my mother looked over her shoulder. "Is she coming after us?"

"I think we're safe," Dad said. He stopped and pointed down the road. "I wonder if they do this every weekend?" he asked.

All along the two-lane highway, cars were parked, transforming the roadside into a giant yard sale. I walked over to a pickup where a young couple sat in the back waiting for customers while watching the Alabama coach Nick Saban's TV show on an iPad. It was a gorgeous day, warm and sunny, and they were both wearing shorts. He had on a Bruce Springsteen T-shirt, and she was wearing an Obama tank top. She looked strong. I asked them if this happened every weekend.

"Nope," she answered, "just two days every year, along Highway 46. You can get some pretty cool stuff."

I looked over their offerings: a few Xboxes, an old lever-action 30-30, a P90X DVD collection, and a shiny gold trombone.

"We already sold some of the good stuff," the woman explained.

"That 30-30 is just like the gun that won the West. Totally cool," the guy said.

"How come you're selling it?" I asked.

She looked over at him, grinning slightly.

"I'm selling it for my dad," he explained, then added, "I was gonna ask him if I could keep it, but I've got plenty of guns, and he said he'd split the money with us."

I nodded at his shirt. "You a Springsteen fan?"

"Yeah, sort of am. I'm into that retro stuff." It's difficult to express how old that made me feel. I nodded toward the girl's Obama tank top.

"Lot of Obama support around here?" I asked. There was something pleasant about the idea of a casual political conversation. I never talked about politics with anyone who didn't work in campaigns.

"Uh-huh," the girl said, completely unimpressed. "I don't really vote," she said, "but I like the shirt."

The guy laughed. "She likes it when people give her a hard time. That's why she wears it."

The girl shrugged and took a drink of the Heineken beer she had been holding to her side. Heineken? "Do they give you a hard time?" I asked. "About the shirt?"

"Nobody around here gives me a hard time about anything. They know I'll bop 'em." She grinned and flexed her sizable biceps.

"Those your folks?" the guy asked, pointing to my mom and dad who were leaning against the Avalon, enjoying the sun.

"Yep. We're Ole Miss fans. Going to the game tonight. My dad and I, anyway."

"He drives?" the girl asked, shading her face to get a better look at my father.

"He does, but I'm driving now."

"How old is he?"

"Ninety-five."

She whistled. "That's awesome."

"He really drives?" the guy asked.

"He does." I started to say more but stopped.

"That's old. Ninety-five. I've got a great-uncle who's ninety-four. But I'd rather lie down in the middle of the interstate at night than let him drive. He drinks a lot. Your dad drink?"

"It's not a big problem." I saw my mother wave to me; time to go. "I should head out. Good luck with selling this stuff."

"Yeah," he said. "If we don't sell the gun, we'll just have to go shoot the crap out of some stuff. That lever action is the coolest thing."

When I got back to the car, my mother asked what we were talking about.

"Guns," I said.

"No surprise," she said.

"This," my father announced, "is excellent fried chicken."

Tuscaloosa is a town of slightly more than 93,000 residents with a stadium that seats over 103,000. The only hotel I could find was about thirty miles outside town, a fancy Marriott built around a golf course. I hoped it would be the sort of place my mother would enjoy while dad and I were at the game.

Traveling with my parents, I'd come to realize the small and larger strains that my mother constantly faced helping my father. He had come to rely on her for almost everything, from suggesting what and where to eat to handling finances. She did it all with grace, but it was unrelenting. For the first time, I found myself thinking I should spend at least part of the year near them so that I could help my mother, if nothing else. I'd been so consumed with my own life that I'd lost focus on what my parents needed. I promised myself that after this football season, I'd rearrange my life to help my parents more, but in the back of my mind I wondered if I was just like an alcoholic telling himself that the next drink would be the last.

At least now I could take comfort in being able to help my mother in little ways, like finding a hotel she might enjoy and giving her time alone when Dad and I went to the games. "I like this," she said as we walked in. The hotel was quiet and had none of the game-day frenzy that we'd found at the Vanderbilt game. The hard-core fans would have planned ahead and stayed closer to the stadium.

We were expecting terrible traffic but easily drove within a couple of blocks of the stadium. Tuscaloosa seemed to have figured out how to get people in and out of town using a combination of one-way streets and an overwhelming presence of city police. Almost every lawn was packed with cars, and the sidewalks were filled with fans dressed in Crimson Tide regalia, tickets in one hand, a beer in the other. The sea of 'Bama fans started about three miles from the stadium and thickened as we drew nearer. We took a right turn, and suddenly the stadium loomed in front of us, huge and extraterrestrial, like a massive spaceship landed in this chipped neighborhood.

Alongside us, fathers and sons walked to the game. "Just like we used to walk to the game," I said, nodding toward a dad who was wearing a sport coat, unusual in a flood of jeans and Alabama T-shirts. "You always wore a sport coat."

Dad smiled. He nodded to a pair of kids who were holding up a cardboard sign that read GAME PARKING, $40. FREE COKE. "Free Coke is a nice touch," he said. We crept along in the slow traffic, and I caught a glimpse of him staring at the stadium, but his thoughts were clearly elsewhere, a look I'd learned to recognize. "I loved playing football," he said, looking out at the scene. "You know why I had to stop at Ole Miss? The training table was eighteen bucks a month. No way I could justify that just to play football." He laughed. "Eighteen bucks. How much did it cost to fill up the car?"

"Sixty-eight."

"And parking is forty bucks. I wasn't great, but I was pretty good," he said.

"If I had it to do over, I'd have kept playing," I said to Dad. Then I asked him something I've always wondered. "When I quit, you never questioned me about it. But would you have liked me to keep playing?"

He looked at me, surprised. "If you had kept playing when you didn't want to and I thought it was because of me, that would have bothered me. You wanted to do other things. You made good grades; you went to college where you wanted to. Those were the things that seemed important, not playing a sport."

It was what I would have expected him to say, and I loved him for it. But I still had regrets, if only because it was something we could have shared. "Me playing, you and Mom coming to games, it would have been fun," I said. "More than fun, special."

He shrugged. "You never know. You might have hated it, you might have gotten hurt, you might have done that instead of thinking about college and be sitting here today regretting that playing football didn't make it possible for you to do what you really wanted to do."

"That's bleak," I said, laughing, but I knew he was right. "You know, sometimes I think I quit playing because I was afraid I wouldn't be good enough to make you really proud. Like I might have let you down."

He put his hand on my shoulder. "That's crazy," he said, and we both sort of laughed, trying to lighten the moment. "You know it's crazy."

We were just a block from the stadium but barely moving in the traffic. My plan was to use the car's handicap sticker—that seemed to have been granted when my dad hit ninety—to snag a spot near the stadium. I rolled down the windows to talk to one of the many police officers in the street. Despite the traffic, everyone seemed in a good mood. This was Saturday, the stadium was within sight, and Alabama was surely about to administer one of its routine ass kickings.

"We're looking for the handicap parking," I said. "The map showed that there was some ahead and to the left?" I waved a printout of the stadium parking scheme from the university's Web site.

The cop was in her thirties, dark-haired and attractive. She stared at me as if I had asked her if Crimson Tide was a laundry detergent.

"You need handicapped?"

"My dad's ninety-five and—"

"Bless your heart," she said to my dad, who waved. "Y'all pull on over."

"Ask her if we park here, if she'll take us the rest of the way," my dad suggested. I'd noticed that he was not shy about asking for help.

The police officer leaned in. She was sweating, and I wondered how long she had been out here. "I got to tell you, these handicap lots fill up fast. You can reserve a place online. You didn't do that, did you?"

"No." I shook my head, feeling like an idiot. Of course. Why did I think that parking at an Alabama–Ole Miss game didn't take advance planning?

"You might find some places if you go up here to the left, go two blocks, then turn right at the first light." She shrugged. "I know that isn't great."

I thanked her, and she waved us back into the slow-moving traffic. I could feel my game excitement start to fade, replaced with a low-grade anxiety. I really should have figured this out better. I knew I had fallen back into a childhood pattern of assuming if it was football, my dad would take care of all the arrangements. He had always planned for the games, bought the tickets, made any arrangements, even years after I was living on my own. We had taken other trips together, like fishing in Alaska, when I handled everything and just sent him the tickets, but he always took charge of any football plans. I'd wanted to spend the fall with my dad to reassure myself that nothing had changed, but of course our time together was doing just the opposite, offering proof that things between us would never be the same. I'd assumed we could recapture those moments of years ago, but on the way to Saturday's stadiums I'd realized just how much time had passed since our first games together. This just made me want to grab each moment a little tighter; after spending so many years in a hurry, I was now pulling hard on time to slow down.

We were directly in front of Bryant-Denny Stadium now. "How many does it seat?" Dad asked as we took in the monstrosity.

"Over a hundred thousand," I said. "One hundred and one thousand and change, actually."

"Superdome is only seventy-five thousand," he said.

"Really? How do you know that?"

He looked at me. "It's a secret?"

I laughed but felt bad because I knew I had fallen into a trap of assuming that he wouldn't know something just because he was ninety-five. I could remember how much I hated that kind of condescension when I was a kid, particularly because I was convinced that I knew everything. Then I'd known that eventually it would end; I could see into the future and imagine being as old as, say, twenty-one. But my father, or anyone past a certain age, could only look ahead and imagine it getting worse. Suddenly it struck me that must be one of the most terrible realities of aging, knowing it changed how you were viewed by the world and with few options to change that perception. Maybe that's what plastic surgery or even younger girlfriends or boyfriends was about, not so much vanity or lust as a deep desire to change how you were viewed by the world. Like when I couldn't remember where the car was parked after the game with Southeast Missouri; if I were my dad's age, anyone would have assumed it was age fogging my memory. There was a line out there just waiting to be crossed when it was no longer vaguely charming to be absentminded but a sign of declining ability, the beginning of a slow walk into senility. For someone like me, who was perfectly capable of losing my keys, wallet, or car or some combination at any given moment and had been that way all my life, the prospects for early senility typecasting seemed particularly bleak.

We tried several parking lots with signs for handicapped spaces. All were full. A block from the stadium in what the locals called the Strip, fans spilled out of bars and restaurants while we watched, stuck in traffic. Two couples in their thirties walked by in Ole Miss garb. This was a "blue" day. "Hotty Toddy!" Dad yelled, waving through the open window.

"Why don't we just get out here and watch it on television," my father said. He nodded toward a restaurant that had multiple televisions tuned to the game. He suddenly sounded tired. "All this traffic."

We were drowning in cars and people, and he seemed overwhelmed. I'd felt that way years ago on Halloween night at Tiger Stadium, the first time my father took me to an out-of-town game: the people, the costumes, the noise, not knowing how it all made sense. Then he had pulled me closer and told me that it was "just football," and everything made sense. But what could I do now to comfort him as he had done for me?

"Do you remember," I asked, "when you went to the Ole Miss–Alabama game in Birmingham? When Archie was playing. When was that . . . ?"

"Nineteen sixty-nine." He thought for a moment, starting to relax as he slipped into memory's river and began to float downstream. "It was October. First weekend, I think."

I quickly pulled up the date on my phone. No reason not to; we weren't moving. Damned if he wasn't right. "October 4, 1969. Why didn't I go?"

"That I can't remember. School, I guess."

"Totally unfair."

"Or maybe a girlfriend." He looked over at me with a smile. That was more likely the truth. From the time I'd hit high school, girls had become more important than football. I wish it hadn't been the case, but it was, and there was no denying it. I'd discovered that while certain girls would like you only if you were a football star, there was this other, larger group that couldn't have cared less; the ones I found most appealing thought it all too typical to go out with a jock. Being a really good football player was hard and involved considerable pain and sacrifice. If there were beautiful girls who preferred you didn't go through all that, well, that made it all the easier to walk away from the sport.

"You know, that might have been the best game I ever saw," Dad said.

We had moved a couple of blocks and were stuck again. In the distance, I could see the iconic statue of Bear Bryant. He seemed to be smiling at my stupidity. I turned out of the traffic, away from the stadium, and toward the campus.

"Good move," my dad said. I didn't tell him I had no idea what I was doing. "Archie was incredible that day. I think he set a record for total yardage."

I pulled behind a redbrick campus building and parked in an empty handicapped space. We weren't very close to the stadium, but I'd given up trying to find anything closer.

"You ought to look it up," Dad said. "How many yards Archie got."

I nodded, wondering how we were going to get over to the stadium. It wasn't that far but a long way for my dad to walk.

"Hey!"

Across the parking lot, a campus security guard was headed our way. My dad looked at me, shaking his head. "Let's just watch this on television."

"Hold on," I told him and got out.

"You can't park here without a specific parking pass," the guard said evenly.

I explained how we had been looking for a handicapped space

and that I'd screwed up by not reserving one in advance and my dad was ninety-five and, well, I laid it on pretty thick.

"You guys Ole Miss fans?" he said. "Drove all the way over here?" I nodded. "And you say your dad's ninety-five?"

"Ninety-six in December. We're trying to go to all of the Ole Miss games this season."

He stepped away and spoke into a radio. My dad was out of the car and stretching. Now that we weren't stuck in traffic, it was easier to appreciate that it was a gorgeous day, hot and clear. Dad walked slowly over.

"Hotty Toddy," he said, smiling. "We came to see 'Bama get beat."

The guard laughed. "You came a long way for nothin' then. My boys don't lose much playing in our house."

"Well, that A&M game last year," Dad said.

I looked at him, amazed. "Are you trying to get us arrested?"

The security guard winced. "I have nightmares about that game. Manziel was just unbelievable."

"You should have seen Archie against the Bear in '69," Dad said.

The guard's face lit up. "You go to that game? I've read all about it. I'm going to law school, and then I want to be a sports agent. That game's a legend."

"He didn't take me to that game," I said flatly. That was starting to really bother me.

A double-cab pickup with the University of Alabama logo on the side pulled up. A fellow large enough to have played defensive tackle for Alabama stuck his head out.

"I heard somebody wants to see a little football?"

"Y'all get in," the guard said. "He'll take you over to the game."

I held out my hand, surprised at how much relief I felt. "That's really good of you. Particularly after my dad was giving you a hard time."

"You know," he said as we were getting into the pickup, "Ole Miss lost that game even with Archie Manning."

My father nodded. "One point," he said, wincing, as if it had happened the day before. "One point."

"Roll Tide," the large driver said with a smile.

"Hotty Toddy," Dad answered.

The original Alabama stadium was built in 1929, and various renovations have since transformed it into one of the most intimidating stadiums for visiting teams in the nation. The noise of a crowd of more than 100,000 was shocking, like falling into a cold lake, a deafening wall of sound that started at the very top seats and gained in power and force until it crested on the field. Everywhere there were reminders that Alabama was one of the great powerhouses in the history of college football, and whoever you were, your destiny of defeat was assured. It started with the Bryant statue in the front of the stadium and continued with relentless videos of past moments in Alabama's football history: twenty-seven conference championships, fifteen national championships, sixty-one bowl games. On this field, the Bear had coached Joe Namath. The message was clear: Alabama is a giant, you are small, submit to your fate.

We found our seats, guided by helpful fans who looked at our Ole Miss shirts with more pity than anger. Thanks to StubHub, we had seats in the first row. Everyone seemed to be going out of their way to be welcoming.

"You know why they are so nice?" Dad asked in a low voice as we got settled. "It's because they know they are going to win."

There was a moment, a not very long moment, when it looked as if all things might be possible on this late Saturday afternoon. Ole Miss received, and the first play was a beautiful Bo Wallace pass to Laquon Treadwell for thirty-eight yards. Then three plays for a fourth and two on the Alabama twenty-nine-yard line, perfect position for a high-percentage field goal.

"Kick," my father murmured. "Take the points. It's Alabama." But Coach Hugh Freeze didn't even seem to consider a field goal. He had a gambler's streak, and Ole Miss was coming into the game undefeated. They could get two yards.

But they didn't. The Alabama defense stuffed them with a one-yard gain. The stadium erupted. My father and I groaned. It's the little moments like this that become game-turning points. I immediately had a bad feeling and felt worse for having it, as if I had let my own team down.

In eight plays, Alabama drove to the Ole Miss eighteen-yard line. Two short passes and six rushing plays, nothing fancy. This was like arm wrestling. No tricks or deception, just a quick test of who was stronger. It was all about the line of scrimmage, and on every play Ole Miss got pushed back by the huge, confident Alabama offensive line, which methodically did its work.

When Ole Miss eventually stopped Alabama and forced them to kick a field goal, it felt like a victory. All those years of games with my dad had taught me the lesson all true fans painfully learn, that the essence of sport is disappointment masked by periodic bursts of joy and nurtured by denial. No one is spared. Fans learn to negotiate their way through games, a useful practice in life. The pain of any moment can be balanced against imagining how much worse it could be. So if Ole Miss was unable to score in the first half, we were celebrating that Alabama hadn't been able to score a touchdown, even if they had made three field goals. To go into the half trailing Alabama by nine to zip is a mere trifle. Like Monty Python's Black Knight: "'Tis just a flesh wound."

We stood and stretched at the half, venturing out to the track that surrounded the field. It felt like all those film scenes of the Roman Colosseum, from *Spartacus* to *Gladiator*, when the crowd was pulling for the lions. "This," Dad said, "is really something."

On the second play of the second half, the great Alabama back T. J. Yeldon ran sixty-eight yards for a touchdown. "He made it look easy," Dad said, wincing. And it was true.

The score was 16-0 when Ole Miss drove to the Alabama six-yard line. They faced a fourth and two, a repeat of their first possession of the game, when they had been in field goal range but opted to go unsuccessfully for the first down. Surely they had learned their lesson and would kick a field goal. It was only the third quarter, and any kind of score would lift their confidence. But being stopped for a first down this close to the goal line and not getting any points would be catastrophic.

And, of course, that's exactly what happened. Ole Miss went for the first down and failed. The stadium seemed to levitate with the roar.

The rest of the game never improved. A perfect Alabama punt put the ball on the Ole Miss one-yard line. On the next play, a safety blitz trapped Wallace behind the line of scrimmage in the Ole Miss end zone. A safety. At that point, the two points were meaningless. It was the humiliation.

My dad looked at me. "Brutal," he said.

"Brutal."

It ended 25–0. Games like this that began with so much hope were devastating. We walked all the way back to the car. It took about forty-five minutes; we'd amble about twenty-five yards, then stop and rest a bit. Behind us, the stadium glowed and still exploded with sound. It was a warm night that felt like so many I'd known growing up. In a driveway, five boys, maybe ten or eleven years old, played football. They were tackling each other on the hard concrete. How many nights had I spent like that?

We lived on a dead-end street in the Belhaven neighborhood of Jackson. My mother and father had built the house the year after I was born, and we lived there until my sister and I both had moved out and they were empty nesters. My aunt and my grandmother lived alongside us. My aunt had been married to my father's older brother, my dad's hero. When he died at forty from complications of childhood rheumatic fever, my aunt went back to work teaching junior high science. She never remarried.

My best friend, Al Stuberfield, lived just down the street. He had a tree house where we spent most of our time; his older brother, Steve, who had suffered brain damage at birth, was our constant companion. He was fiercely strong, fearless, and gentle as a drowsy cat unless he felt his brood had been threatened; then he was capable of great acts of terrifying intimidation.

Once we were playing football with some older kids from St. Mary Street in a vacant lot across the street from Al's house. One of them didn't like how hard Al tackled him—he was a tough tackler—and pushed Al when he got up. You've seen these sorts of phony playground fights a million times: kids pushing each other, nobody wanting to take a swing.

In a flash, Steve charged across the street and lifted the older kid over his head as if he were a cardboard cutout. He twirled him around in circles. It was so sudden and so spectacular that after a few breathless moments everyone had to laugh, including the kid being given the ride. After a bit, Steve put him down, both a little dizzy. He looked at us and Al told him thanks, and Steve went back across the street, duty done.

"Why don't we get him to play?" one of the older guys said, awestruck. "I want him on my team."

"He doesn't like to play football," Al said.

"Why not?"

"He doesn't like to hit people."

Everybody laughed except Al and me. We knew it was true.

In Jackson in the 1960s, the city ran trucks through neighborhoods spraying a toxic DDT mix to kill mosquitoes. We all considered it great fun to run behind the trucks and dart in and out of the mist like schooling fish. Al and I and a couple of guys from the neighborhood once played most of a football game while running behind the slow-moving monsters. Later I read that the city backed up the trucks to the Jackson jail during the Freedom Riders days and sprayed the DDT into cells. There were times running behind the trucks that we'd get too close and the mist would burn our eyes and throats. But we could move in and out and stay as far back as we wanted. Being trapped inside a cell with no escape must have been terrible.

It had been like that one June night in 1963, running behind the mosquito truck, tossing a football, talking about the Rebels. We ran behind it all the way up Piedmont Street, our street, to Riverside, where it turned. We walked and ran back, throwing passes to each other, coughing some after the truck's mist.

Our house was almost at the end of the street, just as it dead-ended into a short bit of dirt road before ending at a creek. That makes it sound as though we were out in the country, which we weren't, but that creek and the bit of woods surrounding it were a hidden world for me for years. Every kid who finds those secret spaces lives a separate life within those boundaries.

Our house sat on a little rise and had brick steps to the front door. I ran up, dodging phantom tacklers all the way. I walked in and shouted that I was home.

My dad came out of the kitchen. He was wearing a plaid robe over pajamas. He put his arm around me and sort of hugged me. My sister was spending the night at a friend's. "You have fun?" he asked in a tired voice.

Something was wrong. I just nodded, and we walked toward the kitchen. My room was just down the hall to the left, past the kitchen. My mother was sitting at the kitchen table, red-eyed. She smiled when she saw me and got up and hugged me. This was not the usual greeting after I walked in covered in dirt, sweat, and a little DDT. All of a sudden I felt like crying.

"What's wrong?" I asked.

"Some bad people did a terrible thing tonight," my dad said.

"What happened?"

He hesitated. "Someone was killed," my mother said.

"Who was it?" I said, and I think I did start to tear up. Killed?

"No one we really knew, but a good man."

"We didn't know him?"

My mother shook her head and started to cry. Dad walked me out and down the short hall to my room. "Mom okay?" I asked.

"It's just sad," he said.

"I'm really sorry. I'll pray for the man tonight." I said prayers most nights.

My father nodded. "That would be good."

We got down by the bed, side by side, with lowered heads as my father prayed, "Our Heavenly Father, tonight we ask you to rest the soul of a Mississippian who was taken by violence. We ask for understanding and forgiveness for those who did this terrible act and for the peace that passes all understanding for the Evers family in their terrible hour of need. In God's name, we pray. Amen."

"Amen," I said.

We stayed like that for a moment, then my dad got up and I got up.

"What was the man's name?" I asked. "Who was killed?"

"Mr. Evers. Mr. Medgar Evers."

"What happened?"

My father hesitated. "He was shot."

"Shot? Did they catch the people who did it?"

"Not yet. But they will."

It took thirty-one years to convict Byron De La Beckwith.

5

Back at Ole Miss, there was a notice in the student union about events commemorating the fifty-year anniversary of Medgar Evers's assassination. It was sponsored by the William Winter Institute for Racial Reconciliation. It startled me to see "50th Anniversary" in print. Time was so strange. It was half a century later, but I could still slip into that moment and relive it. Years would go by without its crossing my mind, and then there it was. It was probably like that for the whole state, for this society called Mississippi. Not just that one horrible murder, but that whole awful, troubled history of blacks and whites.

My parents and I had moved into the hotel on the Ole Miss campus, and I'd been spending a lot of time in the student union after discovering it had all the critical food groups, from Pinkberry yogurt to Chick-fil-A. The union looked like its counterpart at most every college campus I'd been on in the past twenty years: long-haired kids, short-haired kids, students who looked as if they were on their way to a party and students in sweatpants, athletes, nerds, black, white, Asian. A gay student association table was passing out information under a sign that read WHEN DID YOU DECIDE YOU WERE STRAIGHT?

A lounge area in the student union overlooked the Grove; students hung out in groups to study or catch naps or argue

Dad's Ole Miss
Hall of Fame photograph

quietly with a boyfriend or girlfriend. Along one wall hung a series of photographs, mostly black-and-white, oddly formal in the scattered-couch-and-overstuffed-chair frat house feel of the space.

These were Ole Miss Student Hall of Fame portraits from each year dating back to 1930. The half a dozen or so from each class stared out with the frozen intensity of the past. My father was here, class of 1941, black-haired, easy smile, absurdly handsome. A couple of years after him, there was another, more intense portrait, less classically handsome, more sharp edges: William Winter.

I stared at Winter's portrait, wondering if the twenty-year-old face of 1943 had any inkling of what was ahead. He had changed my life, but that could be said by everybody in that student union. They just hadn't been given the chance to understand it as I had.

When asked why I was drawn to campaigns, I never really tell the truth, if only because so few would understand. How do you explain the power of one foggy night in a Mississippi high school football locker room listening to grown men talk about the odds that one of them might be killed?

It was 1967 and still the Mississippi Burning season, just four years after Medgar Evers had been assassinated. William Winter, a family friend whom my parents knew from Ole Miss, was running in the Democratic primary for governor as the moderate on race. My parents were trying to help.

Winter was running against a congressman who had lost an arm in World War II, John Bell Williams. Williams was the "seg" candidate, as everybody said back in those days. On this night, Winter was waiting to talk to a big rally of supporters gathered on a high school football field on Mississippi's Gulf Coast. There had been death threats, explicit ones: if you speak tonight, you will be shot.

There was no Secret Service, of course, or any formal security at all. My father, a former FBI agent, was among a loosely assembled group of volunteer law enforcement types, both retired and active. They had gathered to try to help Winter, who was unassuming but with a country toughness impossible to intimidate.

Surrounded by the larger men, Winter cut a slim, straight figure with an unnatural erectness. I'd watched him in this campaign and realized that he carried himself the same way football players did when they got up from injuries and walked back to the bench, eager to show that the hit didn't hurt, head high, even though everyone knew it did.

At barely fifteen years old, I could do little more than sit there quietly and take in this scene of quiet courage, as warm-up speakers got the crowd roaring. I sat off to the side, trying to be invisible, worried someone would ask me to leave. I felt terribly privileged and grown up. It was as though a door had been opened between adolescence and adulthood. Much effort and money and, yes, love had been expended shielding me from the uglier side of life, but here I was glimpsing a hint of it, and no one was covering my eyes or trying to paint it with prettier colors than it deserved. Had I not won life's lottery being born to loving parents in a comfortable world, I no doubt would have seen this earlier. I'd have grown up faster, harder, tougher. Watching these brave men make hard choices made me begin to realize just how sheltered I was. Despite all the efforts to mold me into a successful product of a value system that called good grades and high test scores "success," my softness was painfully apparent to me.

The men were all imploring Winter not to speak, but he was insistent. Finally, Winter just held up his hands—a gesture I'd seen him make many times—and said, "Boys, I'm gonna give my speech." That was it. The finality in his voice was something they understood. One of the men went out to a car and came back with a bulky bulletproof vest. With a sigh, Winter agreed to wear it and began strapping it on while his wife tried not to cry.

Some of the men tried to hide rifles and handguns under their coats. My father didn't carry a gun; at least I don't think he did. He hated guns. Winter started to go out, but one of the men pulled him back by the shoulders, and they said the Lord's Prayer together in low voices. Then Winter turned and went out, silhouetted in the light, a perfect target. A few steps later, a couple of the largest men followed, their guns shielded from sight. Then my father walked out with Mrs. Winter and another man.

Winter survived that night but lost the election. Years later he would find another moment and win. Me, I was hooked. What could be greater than watching a brave man go out and put his life on the line to win in the name of what he believed was right?

I walked precincts for Winter that summer in 1967, knocking on doors and leaving door hangers. My mother traveled some with his wife, Elise, and sometimes I'd get to go to events, where I'd hand out brochures and say, "Vote for Winter!" I'd been doing that one morning, early, at a shift change at the Pascagoula shipyard, and a lean fellow in his twenties grabbed me by my nice sport shirt and pulled me close. "I wouldn't vote for that nigger-loving son of a bitch if God almighty asked me to." His friends laughed and pushed him along, one slapping me on the back and saying, "Sorry, kid, he had a rough night." I'd like to say I pushed him back or challenged him, but I just stood there, taking it.

That 1967 election was also the one in which Byron De La Beckwith ran for lieutenant governor of Mississippi. He had been tried twice for the killing of Medgar Evers, both trials ending in hung juries. He used that publicity to launch his political campaign for lieutenant governor.

Beckwith's slogan: "He's a straight shooter." He came in fifth with just over 34,000 votes.

I turned fifteen during that election, and by then I already had a complicated relationship with my Mississippi identity. I was nine when I first left the state for any extended period, a two-month stint at a camp in the North Carolina mountains. That was the first of five summers spent at the same camp, and even then I think I understood it was intended to be more than just a fun place to spend the summer but also an entry ramp to a different world. The camp selected by my parents, which really meant my mother, was called Camp Yonahnoka in Linville, North Carolina, at the base of Grandfather Mountain. It was owned and run by an ancient Mr. Chips sort of figure from Episcopal High School in Alexandria, Virginia. And that was the key. It wasn't so much a summer camp as a training ground for Episcopal. The counselors were almost all EHS students or graduates, and it was run like a mini-EHS, with the day divided into the same breaks as class times using the same bell-ringing codes. It was inevitable I'd want to go to EHS.

My parents couldn't afford a camp like Yonahnoka, but my mother helped pay for it by working as a camp representative, giving presentations around Mississippi, Alabama, and Louisiana. Yonahnoka sent her slides of the camp with Grandfather Mountain towering in the background. There was a clear, alpine lake at the camp as different from my Mississippi brown swimming holes as a High Latin Mass from a deep-woods Pentecostal service.

My mother was good. She used the same skills that helped her launch the Kappa Kappa Gamma sorority at Ole Miss: pure charm and a quick laugh that always put her at the center of any comedic misfortune. She was beautiful but seemed unaware of her beauty, which, of course, only made her more compelling. Watching her whip through the exotic slides of this faraway place in the mountains was like traveling a wormhole to another universe.

At the end, when she talked about what the campers were

expected to bring and said that a warm jacket was needed for the cold nights of July, the gathered would murmur in delight and disbelief. "But the camp provides all the blankets the boys will need. Can you imagine, sleeping under blankets in July with no air-conditioning? That's about as close to heaven on earth as I imagine we'll see," she'd say with a laugh, and, man, let me tell you, every single person left thinking about the deadening heat of Mississippi in July.

I can remember how excited she was when she came into my room one night to tell me that enough families had committed to sending their sons that I'd be able to go. Maybe it's my imagination or maybe it's what I think the truth was, but there seemed to be more than just a sense of happiness; there seemed to be a sense of relief. You can get out.

That I had this chance was a pure accident of my birth, being lucky enough to have parents who gave me options. We say that in America anyone can become anything he desires, which is probably more true for us than most countries, but that still doesn't make it true. And nowhere in America have circumstances of birth been more defining than Mississippi. With my parents, I won the lottery: loving parents, every possible advantage, and, yes, born white. All Mississippi stories are eventually about race, and mine is no exception. The path of my life wasn't fully determined the day I was born, but the choices I might be afforded were certainly a gift of birth and nothing I had earned.

Earlier that year at my father's ninety-fifth birthday party given by his old law firm, I found myself trying to express this to someone I had known all my life: Alonzo Kent, the son of Elzoria Kent, who had worked for my family until well after I had left for college. Alonzo and his sister had nursed Elzoria through a long decline with great love. He had worked for the law firm for years in various office management and support areas.

It had been years since we'd seen each other. We hugged. To my surprise, I found myself trying not to choke up. We grabbed a table in one of the law firm's conference rooms, an oddly formal place for a conversation best had over beers on a back porch. "You know, you're looking a lot like your mom," I said.

"That's just what a guy likes to hear," he said, laughing. "But I know it's the truth."

And then we talked about his mom. "I don't have any memories before Elzoria," I told him. "She's there, in my head, from the start."

"Me too," Alonzo said, smiling.

We talked about Elzoria and the special way she had of laughing and how positive she had been even when there was darkness in her life. I struggled to tell him what she meant to me. "I remember once, I came home and I was complaining about something. I can't remember what. Something stupid, I'm sure. I was maybe eight years old. She got right in my face—"

He laughed. "Oh yeah. I know that."

"And she told me, 'Stuart Stevens, you are the luckiest boy in this whole wide world, and don't you ever start feeling sorry for yourself.'" Alonzo smiled, trying not to notice that I was tearing up. "She said, 'Your mama and daddy love you and Jesus loves you and Elzoria loves you and that's all any boy in this world could need. You hear me now?'"

Alonzo smiled. "That sounds like her. Yes, sir," he said, both of us drifting back in memory.

"I always wanted her to be proud of me," I said.

"You know she was," Alonzo said, waving his hand, as if to brush off any notion otherwise.

We sat there for a long moment. "She didn't have an easy life, I know, Alonzo. But she touched so many people."

"We were blessed to have her," he said, squeezing my hand. Christ, I thought, she's his mother, and he's comforting me. How selfish can I be?

We talked some about football and Jackson-area players who were up at Ole Miss. It was time to go, but I kept vamping because there was something I wanted to say to him but wasn't sure I knew the right words. Finally, when he said he had to get back, I couldn't put it off.

"Look, Alonzo, once, when I was a kid, I heard your mother say something to my mom that has kind of haunted me all these years. My mom, too, when we talk about it."

He looked at me with a questioning smile.

"I don't know what they had been talking about, but she said, 'You know, Mrs. Stevens, I think if I had been born white, I could have really been something.'"

Alonzo sighed. "My mom said that?"

I nodded. He turned away for a moment, and we were both tearing up. He came back with a slight smile. "She was something."

Like a lot of big-time college schools, Ole Miss had spent a fortune building posh athletic facilities, ostensibly for all the student athletes but focused on the moneymaking marquee football teams. The new Manning Center was next to the stadium and connected by an underground passage so the players could emerge into the stadium tunnel directly from the locker room. It had weight rooms, an indoor practice field, and team meeting rooms. I'd been dying to get a peek inside the place, and before the Texas A&M game I got the chance.

It happened because Mitt Romney was visiting Ole Miss for the game. One of his closest aides during the campaign, Garrett Jackson, was a former student equipment manager while an undergrad at Ole Miss. After eighteen months of listening to Garrett and me talk about our passion for the Rebels, Mitt had decided he had to come to a game and see for himself.

All through the campaign, even at the most stressful moments, Garrett had shown a preternatural calm. I finally asked him how he could be so steady, particularly in his first campaign at a young age. "I can promise you," he said, "that nothing we've done can come close to what it's like to be standing on the sidelines of an SEC football game having a coach scream at you because you brought the wrong kicking shoe. This running-for-president stuff is easy compared to the SEC."

Garrett had arranged for Mitt to visit the Manning Center, and my dad and I were able to tag along. As much as I wanted to see the new facilities, I still had a certain PTSD shiver at the thought of yet another locker room. We'd had more than twenty debates in the campaign, and it seemed as if most of them were on college campuses that used locker rooms for holding spaces before the debates. But the new Ole Miss facility was like nothing we had encountered on the debate circuit.

"This," my father announced, "is like a fancy country club, not a locker room."

He was absolutely right. It was high ceilinged, with wide wood-grained lockers. WIN THE DAY was emblazoned over and over on the lighting panels that hung between the rows of lockers. Larger-than-life action photographs depicted Rebel greats, past and present.

One photograph was of early Ole Miss football great Bruiser Kinard. "We were good friends," my dad said, pointing to Bruiser's black-and-white photograph, which showed a stern, handsome young man in a white jersey. He had high cheekbones and carefully combed hair as if he was going out of his way to disavow his nickname, Bruiser.

"You knew Bruiser Kinard?" Garrett asked. It was one of the few times I had heard him sound impressed.

Bruiser was Ole Miss's first all-American and had played professional football for the very baseball-sounding Brooklyn Dodgers and New York Yankees. He was a running back, defensive lineman, and kicker and in the entire 1936 season missed only twelve minutes of playing time.

"We played together when I was on the freshman team at Ole Miss," my dad said, "and I saw him play in New York after we graduated."

"That is something," Garrett said, nodding. He looked at my father as if he were meeting the oldest Confederate widow, someone with a living tie to an unimaginable era.

We walked out of the locker room into a training area where Mitt was meeting some of the athletic trainers and equipment managers. He gestured around the athletic fantasy world.

"Was it like this when you were at Ole Miss?" Mitt asked my dad, laughing. They had met once before on the campaign trail when we had ended up in Asheville. My mother had driven my dad to the airport, and the idea was that I would drive their car in our little motorcade while we were in Asheville.

In honor of the occasion, my mother had finally taken off her fading Obama bumper sticker from 2008. The local Asheville advance team had very kindly positioned my parents' battered Toyota in the motorcade. When we arrived, to my horror, my mother informed me that she was very excited about driving in the motorcade.

"You don't really understand how they drive in these crazy motorcades," I said. "They can go sort of fast, and if they close the road, they do this swerving thing sometimes."

"That sounds like fun."

"Let's put it this way," I said. "I'd feel safer if al-Qaeda were chasing us with RPGs than you driving this Toyota at eighty miles per hour." Truth was, I'd never driven in a motorcade before either, and I was nervous about my driving. As it turned out, I did a miserable job, and the Secret Service crew gave me a hard time about it for the rest of the campaign.

Later that day, before a rally in downtown Asheville, we had ended up in a holding room for more than an hour. My plan was for my parents to meet Mitt and then I'd take them into the rally. But the quick meeting had turned into a long conversation about the South, differences between North Carolina and Mississippi, and George Romney, whom my parents had much admired. I watched it all a little nervously, suggesting several times that we should go, but I was waved off.

Afterward, Mitt said to me, "You're so lucky to have them. So lucky."

That Saturday at Ole Miss was one of the designated days that potential recruits could visit the campus. The NCAA heavily regulates all contact between colleges and high school recruits in a byzantine system where good intentions seem often pushed to absurd levels. Each college is allowed only one official visit by a recruit, so the pressure to maximize each visit is huge. The recruits and their families had been invited to spend the afternoon touring the new athletic facilities before the game.

At the end of one of the training rooms, there was a display of the various combinations of game-day uniforms for the 2013 season. As anyone who has watched college or professional football lately knows, there seems to be something of a competition among some teams as to who can have the most embarrassing uniforms. It's as if a marketing study were done that concluded that the sport would undergo massive growth proportional to the regrettable color schemes and designs of uniforms.

Fortunately, Ole Miss had the good sense or good fortune to stay with classic looks: red jersey and white pants; white pants and white jersey with blue trim; all blue pants and jersey with white trim (my favorite); blue pants and white jersey with blue trim; and blue pants with red jersey and white trim. They all had the benefit of making those who wore them look like football players and not failed fashion experiments. Along with these came an impressive shoe collection with different cleats for different conditions, various gloves, and color-coordinated pads of every variety: elbow and arm pads, shoulder pads, hip pads, knee pads, back pads.

"So, every player gets all this stuff?" asked a tall high school recruit who had come up behind my father and joined us in marveling at the gear.

"You have to be good when you wear this gear," my father said, chuckling.

"I feel fast just looking at it," the recruit said, smiling. "Man, how much you think all that stuff cost?"

"Nothing you have to worry about," my father said.

"At my high school, we have to pay for some of our gear," the kid said. "I worked an extra job last summer so I could look good on the field."

"I bet you did look good," my father said.

The recruit smiled. "We haven't lost a game yet."

"You gonna play for the Rebels?" I asked.

He frowned. "I can't commit now, you know. I've got to do this by the rules. That's what everybody keeps telling us. I don't want to screw anything up."

"We're just fans and hope we get to see a play on Saturdays."

He relaxed, smiling. "I think if my mama saw me playing on television, she'd have a heart attack."

"Well, you know what that means," my father said. "She'll just have to come to every game."

The kid smiled as if he just signed a multimillion-dollar contract. "Man, wouldn't that be something. I just want to be a Sunday player. Take care of her."

A "Sunday player" was slang for playing in the NFL. "I hope it all works out," I said, shaking his hand but wondering if he had any idea of what lay ahead and the daunting odds for success. Even for the scholarship elite players, the odds of injury were great and the chance for NFL riches remote. Division One schools with major programs made vast sums off the football teams, and while the players were given scholarships, they had no chance to participate in any of the wealth they were helping generate. It was an inherently unfair, deeply flawed system, but a perfect solution was elusive. The notion of giving players some profit sharing of the revenue they generated or paying them large salaries would abandon any pretext of a dividing line between amateur and professional sports. At the very least, it seemed to me that players should be paid something for the forty hours a week during the season a big-time program demanded. Even if they made the same per hour as students working in the cafeteria or school store, it would help. Some of the kids had absolutely no money, and over and over players got into trouble for taking small gifts of what amounted to petty cash. And the concept that a university could charge for a player's likeness on a jersey but a kid couldn't sell his own autograph struck me as utterly insane and deeply unfair. It was an invitation for cheating.

"You enjoy playing," Dad told the recruit, "but get your degree. You'll need that."

"Yes, sir. My mother says the same thing."

"You'll make her real proud," Dad said, and the kid beamed.

We left him looking at the uniforms, probably dreaming of what it would be like to run through the tunnel to the screams of the crowd.

"I hope he makes it," Dad said. "I really do."

To get to the game, we walked the same route the players took every day for practice: out of the Manning Center and up the surprisingly steep stairs to the beautifully groomed fields that lay in the shadow of the Vaught-Hemingway Stadium. It was dusk, the setting sun cast a soft glow on the green fields. Behind us, thousands streamed into the stadium with that expectant hope that comes with a new Saturday and a 0–0 scoreboard.

Young kids played out fantasies on the practice field while their parents had one more drink and tried to conjure up the energy of past triumphs. From inside the stadium came the collage of sounds that preceded every game: the slick videos that pumped the crowd for the battle to come, the band playing its medley of songs that included an homage to Dixie, the cheers and outbreaks of loud "Hotty Toddy" chants.

We stood there for a few minutes while my father caught his breath after the walk up the stairs, soaking in the scene. "You know," I said, "I don't think there's anyplace I'd rather be right now."

My father nodded, and we watched the kids. On a night like this, with the stadium full and glory waiting to be seized, I wondered if anyone who ever played football didn't wish he were still playing. It was the perfect dream of youth, to be young and strong and full of promise and on that field.

The sky grew a little darker and the air just a touch cooler.

"Hey," I said, "let's go. We don't want to miss the kickoff."

It took one play to make it clear why Texas A&M's Johnny Manziel had won the Heisman Trophy as a freshman. He took the snap from his usual position five feet back from the center, did a little pump fake, and then just juked and jived straight up the field. Watching it reminded me of when I used to box and got hit for the first time by an exceptional puncher. I wasn't a very good boxer and got hit a lot. Most punchers were predictable in their power, but occasionally somebody came along who hit with a shot that immediately signaled this was not going to be fun. So it was with Manziel: one play, one player touching the ball, seventeen-yard gain. There was no huddle; this was speed football, the sort that Ole Miss's coach, Hugh Freeze, loved to play. Strike fast. Don't let the defense get settled. Keep them rattled.

With the sort of ease that signaled "I could do this all night, folks," Manziel kept the ball, swiveled his hips right and left in half spins, and was nine yards down the field before he was touched. The effortless grace of his play sucked the energy out of Ole Miss.

My father and I sighed. Ole Miss had lost to Alabama at the game we'd attended and then lost the following week to Auburn, which we didn't make. The weather report had been nasty for the game, and Dad had felt like resting up. So they were now 3-2 for the season, and this was looking like a very long night. My dad shrugged. "That Manziel, he's like a big cat that can pass. If he has the ball last, we'll lose." Like all great fans, my father had strong opinions; certainty was an essential quality in a fan. There was no joy in liking a team; no bliss in not caring for an opponent. You had to love your team and hate your rivals to be a true fan, and, most important, you must always have the certainty, without a doubt, that you know what is best for your team. If the confidence in your convictions starts to slip, best to just admit that you were once a fan but are now only an observer, another window-shopper without either the money or the need to buy.

At the half, the Ole Miss defense had somehow held Manziel to fourteen points, which seemed a small miracle given his talents. In a choppy give-and-take, the Ole Miss offense had scored one touchdown. It was 14–10.

"I'll take that," my father said, standing up and stretching as the Ole Miss "million-dollar band" was heading onto the field. "You know I'm ninety-five and get these things mixed up, but I seem to remember there was ice cream here."

We had been invited to watch the game in one of the stadium's new skyboxes by a friend of mine who also worked in my father's law firm. Outside in the hallway, there was a freezer of ice cream that had caught my dad's eye when we stepped off the elevator.

The Rebel fans around seemed upbeat, despite being behind. "When it's 14–10, everybody still thinks they can win," Dad said.

"It's like being forty," I said.

He paused and thought about it for a moment. "I can't really remember, but that sounds right." We made our way over to the magic ice cream freezer. Half a dozen kids, seven or eight years old, were playing football in the wide hallway. Dad opened up the freezer and brought out a couple of different kinds of ice cream sandwiches, instantly bringing the kids' game to a halt.

"How much does the ice cream cost?" a blond girl who was a little taller than any of the boys asked.

"Doesn't cost a thing," Dad said. "You want some?"

So my dad became the Ice Cream Man, spreading out the various choices and handing them out to the football players.

"You remember Seale-Lily ice cream?" I asked him. Seale-Lily was a local ice cream brand when I was growing up.

"Of course." He thought for a minute. "You eat it with a smile," he said, conjuring up its long-ago slogan.

"Yes! I can't believe you remember that."

"Don't know why not. I was eating a lot more Seale-Lily a lot longer than you."

That was true. "Do you remember that guy who used to do their ads on WJTV? He was a weatherman and the news guy."

My father thought for a while, then shook his head. "I don't think so. What did he look like?"

"That's the best part! He was bald and used to go on television eating ice cream cones, talking about how great the ice cream was. When I was a kid, I thought he looked like an ice cream cone."

When I had been these kids' age, WJTV and WLBT had dominated television in Mississippi. Those stations combined with *The Clarion-Ledger* and the *Jackson Daily News* had largely defined the outside world. WLBT was famous for editing national newscasts whenever it disliked the coverage of civil rights. Back in the 1950s, when Thurgood Marshall appeared on an NBC news show, WLBT blocked it out with a sign that read CABLE DIFFI-CULTY. Later the station became the only one in the country to have its license revoked for overt racism. But now, not so much later, the stands were filled with blacks and whites cheering blacks and whites on the field.

Nelson Mandela had shrewdly used rugby to unify South Africa. In many ways, football, high school and college, had played the same role in the South. On Friday nights and Saturday afternoons, blacks and whites had discovered what it felt like to be on the same side. Instead of trying to keep blacks out, universities waged fierce recruiting battles to attract black athletes. Now if violence was to break out over a black student entering a southern school, it's most likely to be between two rival coaches fighting over a star athlete.

The football field was a defined space and time in which it was proven over and over that to be successful, everyone must work together and care about each other. Sports had proven the clichés to be true: that only by uniting could we build something greater than ourselves. You could talk all you wanted about why a society should treat races equally, but sports—football—did make the theoretical very real. There was something powerful about the sense of loss and fear when your son's teammate didn't get up from a play or the joy shared with the stranger next to you in the stands after a big team win that made racial differences very small and trite.

It was hard to imagine all the anger and the blood that had been shed over the years in the segregation battles in an effort to avoid . . . what? This? This stadium filled with raucous, happy fans? A student union where blacks and whites ate frozen yogurt together and complained about tests and teachers?

"They have any more of those good hot dogs?" my dad asked, breaking me out of my meditations on race and the past.

"That may be the most important question of the night," I said.

"Let's grab some and get back," Dad said. "Don't want to miss the second-half kickoff."

Ninety-five and still not wanting to miss a single play of a big game. Not a bad life goal.

Ole Miss received the second-half kickoff and promptly went three and out. When the Ole Miss offense clicked, it was a thing of beauty to behold. But like a high-performance sports car, it could be tricky getting it started. They lacked the big power runners to grind downhill and depended on speed and finesse, maximizing the skills of their excellent receivers and small, speedy backs. To work, they needed to establish a rhythm of very quick plays, using shallow screen passes the way more traditional teams would use an off-tackle running dive. If a defense interrupted their rhythms by stopping them on first down or pressuring the quarterback, they seldom were able to adjust.

Johnny Manziel was different. He had that rare ability to convert seeming disaster into shocking success, scrambling all over the field, never giving up. He embraced chaos and played the game with a sandlot improvisation, like a stock car racer who loved to take turns on two wheels. In nine quick plays, he scored, putting A&M up 21-10, and did it with an ease that made it seem he could score at will. My father and I just looked at each other and laughed. It was maddening, but he was so good, so magical, that if you had an ounce of love for the game of football, you had to celebrate Manziel.

When Ole Miss got the ball back, my father leaned forward eagerly, as if he wanted to run out on the field. "We need this," he said, banging his fist against my knee. "We need to score now."

In a methodical fourteen-play drive, alternating quarterbacks, Ole Miss drove down the field and did what they had to do: score. It was what sports announcers have taken to calling "grown-up football": no trick plays, no lucky breaks, no third downs longer than three yards, just solid play.

The problem with scoring against Texas A&M was the disturbing reality that you then had to give the ball back to Johnny Manziel. In nine successive pass plays, he took his team seventy yards to the Ole Miss ten-yard line. It felt like watching a college player thrust into a high school game; Manziel simply played the game at a higher level than anyone else. But then, at the ten-yard line, he unexpectedly made one bad pass, thrown over the middle into the end zone for an easy Ole Miss interception.

My father leaped to his feet and thrust his hands over his head. Below us in the student section, a joyous "Hotty Toddy" broke out. "This is our chance," my father said. "Now we go ahead."

But only three plays later, Ole Miss's quarterback Bo Wallace threw an interception on the Ole Miss twenty-yard line. It was as if fate were just batting us about, a giant cat playing with a somewhat amusing toy.

The last quarter was as brutal and desperately played as any fifteen minutes of football I've ever seen. On both teams, players were felled by injuries, hauled off the field, and replaced by another clean uniform sprinting onto the field.

The intensity and violence on both sides came from playing for something more than numbers on a scoreboard. Battles had been fought all night between individual players, and now it was about proving who could endure pain longer, who could break the other player's will.

Neither team would collapse or give up. With three minutes left, it was tied, 38–38.

Ole Miss got the ball at their twenty-five-yard line, with every Rebel fan in the stadium standing and screaming. This was when the team had to prove they could win. After thirty-eight points, all they needed was one more drive for a score. Then horror unfolded with stunning quickness: one incomplete pass; a second incomplete pass; a third incomplete.

"That's it?" my father moaned. "Three passes? No runs?"

The stadium was suddenly, shockingly quiet as the punting team came out on the field.

The rest of the game felt like standing against the executioner's wall watching the firing squad assemble. Manziel did what he had done all night: he threw for fourteen yards; he ran for twelve yards; he ran for thirteen yards. Then he handed it off to a couple of big backs to take the ball down to the Ole Miss fifteen-yard line with four seconds left. Then he trotted off the field for the field goal kicker, his work done.

If you had told me it would cost ten years of my life for A&M to miss the kick, I would have gladly taken the deal. I think most of the stadium would have as well.

Of course he made the kick.

My father and I stood there sighing. It was a terribly painful way to end a game, but the seven plays it had taken A&M to get in position to kick the field goal had been sort of an emotional hospice care, offering time to prepare for the inevitable.

While the A&M players were mobbed on the field by their fans, the Ole Miss players filed out through the stadium tunnel. A few of the students nearest the tunnel yelled support and began to clap, and then others did. In our box, we joined the students applauding.

But it was a joyless applause. Dying may feel worse than losing a game like this, but at least with dying there's the comfort of knowing it's unlikely to happen again. In the hallway, Cooper Manning, the oldest of the Manning brothers, was consoling Rebel fans like a priest at a funeral. There seemed to be some comfort in being in the presence of a Manning, like a connection to a better time or a reminder that all pain was temporal. A tall, smiling figure with that shock of brown hair, he seemed to radiate the calmness of someone who had known disappointment before—his own career cut short by a near-tragic medical condition—and emerged stronger.

No doubt any objective observers would consider the depression that seemed to afflict every Ole Miss fan shuffling out of the stadium as a gross overreaction. Had Ole Miss just had a bit of better luck and execution and been able to squeeze out those last three points, there would be delirious celebration and all life's problems would suddenly seem far less significant. But that hadn't happened, and now whatever was bothering anyone before the game surely loomed larger. It was difficult to escape that little voice inside shouting: Unlucky. I'm just unlucky. My whole life I've been unlucky. I will always be unlucky.

Three points. It was staggering how three points could change a worldview. My father put his arm around my shoulders. "Next week," he said.

"Next week."

6

My mother's family was from Louisiana. Her mother had been born and raised outside Shreveport on the Rough and Ready Plantation. At eighteen, she ran away with the clarinet player from a band playing at a debutante party. It was not fated to be one of those happily ever after marriages, but it lasted long enough for my mother to be born. The clarinet player was mostly a stranger to my mother until later in life when they both ended up living in Jackson. He ran a music store, and I worked there off and on in high school and loved the time I got to spend with him. He was a Kelly, pure Irish, and a wonderful man.

My grandmother seemed to like marrying, if not being married, and kept at it through five different marriages. She would note, always with a twinkling smile, that she never married the same man twice, though she did marry cousins with the same last name. This proved to be a boon with monograms. Her maiden name was Mary Land. She loved to fish, hunt, and cook and wrote about all three. She was the first female member of the Louisiana Sports Writers Association and wrote a classic of southern eating, *Louisiana Cookery*. As a kid, I wasn't really aware of her writing, but I loved to go fishing with her and listen to her stories of living in Mexico. For a while, she had a lion cub as a pet; that ended predictably when it mauled some overly friendly visitor. She drove a Jaguar XK-E, until the afternoon she flipped it into a bayou during a Louisiana storm. A Good Samaritan dragged her half-drowned from under the ruined car. She had respiratory problems the rest of her life.

My mother was a student at LSU when she transferred to Ole Miss to "colonize" a new chapter of the Kappa Kappa Gamma sorority. It was both an adventure and a paying job. Her mother was between husbands and "none of them as rich as they should've been," as my grandmother would joke.

Before she got on a train to Oxford, my mother's only knowledge of Mississippi was the Gulf Coast, which is like knowing Boston through Cape Cod. Compared with the sophistication of New Orleans, where she had gone to the McGehee School, it must have felt like an exotic Peace Corps posting.

Growing up in a family with LSU and Ole Miss ties, I assumed that the intense rivalry between the schools was a peculiarity of ours, a family feud being acted out in Oxford, Baton Rouge, and Jackson for our benefit. It was only later that I realized that the Ole Miss–LSU football rivalry started in 1894.

When I had first talked to my dad about spending a season going to games together, he had immediately homed in on the rivalry. "When's the LSU game?" he asked. "That will be the biggest. That will be the biggest." He was right. Now the LSU game was six days away, and as the campus began to recover from its A&M near-victory hangover, surely worse than a blowout-defeat hangover, that special "big game" feeling began to take over the university. We spent that week on campus staying at what my parents called the Alumni House, as it had been known for decades. It was the on-campus hotel that had been renovated a few years back and now officially bore the more sophisticated name The Inn at Ole Miss.

"When I was in law school," my father said as we were walking over to the student union for coffee and frozen yogurt, "we talked one of my professors into driving down to Baton Rouge for the LSU game." Dad and I liked to walk over to the student union mid-morning. It wasn't a long distance, but walking with my dad was never fast. For the first time this season, there was coolness in the air, the sort of weather that people mean when they talk about "football weather." In the Northeast and places like Michigan, this can come on late August nights, but in the South, the land of brutal two-a-day practices in August with the temperature over a hundred degrees, football weather was October and November, just as the season started to come into sharp focus.

"Erskine Wells and I talked a law professor of ours into driving down to Baton Rouge after class on Friday." Erskine Wells had gone on to become a World War II hero in the Pacific and lived just down the street from us when I was growing up. "We didn't have a car. The professor did. We told him we'd drive and help with gas if he'd go. Took us forever, but it was a hell of a game. Ole Miss won, and when we were leaving the game walking through the parking lot, there were all these LSU cars with tiger tails on their car antennas. We couldn't believe it, but the professor tried to rip every tail off as we walked back to the car. We were lucky to get out of there alive."

Outside the student union, a fraternity was selling corn dogs with a sign that said LSU CORN DOGS: GAME SPECIAL.

"Corn dogs?" my father asked, puzzled.

"It's a rap on LSU fans," I explained. "Saying they smell like corn dogs."

"Why?"

"It started with an Auburn fan writing something on the Internet about how all the LSU fans smell like corn dogs. It's sort of caught on from there."

My father frowned. "Corn dogs? Not beer or shrimp, but corn dogs?"

"It doesn't make sense," I said. "But people seem to enjoy it."

He stepped up and pulled out his wallet. "We'll take two," he said.

"Hotty Toddy," the frat corn dog vendor said.

"Hotty Toddy," my father agreed. "Only a buck? That's a bargain."

"We want the corn dog experience to spread," the seller explained quite earnestly, as if passing out religious material.

The corn dogs were good. I couldn't remember the last time I had eaten one, and at the moment that seemed to have been a grave mistake.

"Smells like corn dogs?" my father asked, waving his corn dog like a baton. "LSU?"

"That's what they say," I replied, laughing.

I suppose it's reasonable to ask what in the world Mississippians were doing making fun of anyone, including the great state of Louisiana. But that, of course, was the point. It was done with the same note of slightly self-mocking pride that the revelers in the Grove are quick to proclaim: "We may not always win the game, but we never lose the party." When you are the poorest state in the nation and seem to have been since Appomattox, when you have more of what everyone tries to have less of—illiteracy, diabetes, obesity, kidney disease, all the witches' brew of poverty—it's only natural to take some modest pleasures in graces and virtues that can't be plotted on a spreadsheet or the actuary tables of life.

The old saying is that the Mississippi delta begins at the lobby of the Peabody Hotel in Memphis and ends in Yazoo City, Mississippi. Below that invisible line is the Territory of New Orleans. If you grow up in Jackson or farther south, almost surely there is a secret part of your heart—and wallet—that belongs in New Orleans. Before "what happens in Vegas stays in Vegas" was a trademarked lure, it was a reality for generations of Mississippians visiting New Orleans. It was a place you could eat and drink and do all manner of things that you couldn't do in Mississippi. This was where nearly naked women swung out from open bar windows on Bourbon Street to entice customers. The only outrage was to be boring. But to think of New Orleans as merely a free-fire zone for vices is to miss its true power and meaning. After all, you could eat and drink at hunting camps and towns along the Mississippi Gulf Coast that always had a full cafeteria of the usual tasty corruptions from gambling to girls.

What made New Orleans different was its Shangri-La quality: there, hidden behind natural barriers (water, not mountains), was a land where you could not only do different things but be a different person. There was the promise that you could be anybody you wanted to be. At home in Mississippi, our lives were defined ever so precisely by a universe of large and small realities not of our choosing: who our mamas and daddies were, where we went to school, how good we were at the sports that mattered, the fight behind the drive-in that we won or lost, how many times a week we went to church and where, was it a dry county or a wet county, or back when everything was dry from New Orleans to Memphis, did your family know a good bootlegger? Who are your cousins? How many did you have? Did you have every Sunday dinner at your grandmother's?

It's easy to understand why my mother, who had grown up in New Orleans and now found herself in Jackson, always felt a part of her was missing. If you were raised on French bread, you can eat all the Wonder bread in the world and still feel hungry. I had grown up hearing that New Orleans was a magical place. Then, the first time I visited, for the 1964 Sugar Bowl, it snowed the day before the game. It was New Year's Day 1964: my first Sugar Bowl, the first snow I could really remember, and my first trip to New Orleans since I was a toddler.

"You remember that first Sugar Bowl you took me to?" I asked my father when we were sitting in the student union eating a post-corn-dog frozen yogurt. They had a Pinkberry just like the one on Montana Avenue in Santa Monica. Corn dogs and tart frozen yogurt had a nice symmetry.

My father thought for a moment and smiled. "Ole Miss and Alabama. Johnny Vaught and Bear Bryant."

We both smiled at the memory. "The old Tulane Stadium," I said. "You know what I remember about that place? How it would shake when everybody stamped their feet. I thought it was going to come down."

"Much more fun than the Superdome," he said.

For that first Sugar Bowl, we stayed uptown with a childhood friend of my mother's. It was close enough to the stadium at Tulane to walk, which meant it was close enough to hear the crowd. "I loved when we walked to the games," I said. "The way you could hear the crowd and the band in the distance. It was like in those Tarzan movies when he'd be in the jungle and hear the native villages in the distance."

"You can't do that at the Superdome," my father said.

New Year's Day, snow, the game—any one of these would have been a great excuse to party in New Orleans. Put all three together, and it was like a sign from the gods of excess that they must be honored. Of course there was a party at the house where we were staying. There were always parties before the games. People arrived hungover from the night before, desperate for Bloody Marys. I hung out in the kitchen, my normal place at parties. Billy, the college-aged son of my parents' friends, was bartending. He was wearing khakis, beat-up penny loafers with no socks, and a madras button-down shirt. His blond hair was a touch longer than the norm, and he seemed to always have a wry grin.

"You want to help?" he asked.

I was stunned. No one had ever asked me to help make a drink. At my parents' parties, if there was a bartender, he would always slip me the cherries used for drinks or drop one in a Coke for me for an instant Cherry Coke. But making a drink?

"I don't know how," I said, but that didn't matter to Billy. "Course you do. Not like you never seen a drink. You just haven't done it. That's not the same as not knowing how." He talked to me as if he had confidence in me. I'd always wanted an older brother, and this was just how I imagined it would be. He would teach me how to make drinks.

Billy showed me how to make a Bloody Mary, mixing the tomato juice and Worcestershire and lemon.

"Some folks like some Tabasco in their drink," he said, holding up a large bottle. "Give 'em a shot or two if they want it. Just don't get it on your hands. You'll end up rubbing your eyes, and that burns like hell."

He said "hell" casually, as though it were just us guys. "I know what Tabasco is like," I said. I didn't want him to think I didn't know anything. "My dad puts Tabasco on everything."

"There you go," he said, winking at me. "You know the drill." It was like being admitted to a special club. A college girl came in and nodded at me. "Who's your helper, Billy?" she asked.

"Had to bring a pro in. Some serious drinkers around here." They smiled at each other, and when Billy handed me her drink to add vodka, she said, "Go easy on that, hon. You know Billy just wants me to get drunk." She giggled and took the drink, gliding off. She left a hint of perfume.

"She's pretty," I said and was surprised I said it as soon as it came out.

"Very," Billy answered, as if he and I talking about pretty girls were a regular thing. "She has to beat guys away with a stick." I thought about this and didn't really understand the meaning but nodded.

"We need some more beer," Billy announced. "You hold down the fort. I'll be right back."

"You're leaving?" I asked. "What do I do?"

"Just what you've been doing."

If I had been a little more worldly, I might have expressed astonishment that beer could be bought on New Year's Day. But I suppose I just assumed it was coming from the bootlegger, that being the only world I knew. Partygoers, or what Billy called "customers," started to come in and asked for drinks. No one seemed to think it odd that an eleven-year-old was tending bar. But then this was New Orleans.

"Yeah, baby," one man said to me after taking a sip. "Now we're talking." He smacked his lips approvingly. I had no idea how much vodka to add, but when I saw that the more I put in, the more my "customers" seemed to like it, I didn't scrimp. There were a lot of red faces that seemed to get redder as they downed their Bloody Marys. They circled back to me like race cars in a pit stop.

When Billy returned with beer, I was glad to see him.

"We need more of this stuff," I said, holding up a nearly empty vodka bottle.

He laughed, then looked more closely. "What happened to the rest of this?" he asked, looking at the bottle.

A woman I'd made a drink for came into the kitchen holding out her glass. "Can't fly on one wing," she said, looking like the happiest person in the room.

"One?" Billy asked, laughing. "How many wings you had?"

"Oh, just one real good one," she said, giving me a wink. "He mixes a mean drink," she said, and I felt a rush of pride.

Later, when we walked to the game, a lot of people took what they called "go cups," the first time I had heard that description. There was still snow on the ground and a melting, not very large snowman with a Rebel flag stuck in its head.

"Are the Rebels going to win?" I asked my dad.

"Today the Rebels are going to win. Yes, sirree." I didn't doubt it for a second.

Ole Miss hadn't lost a game all season, though they had tied two games, which seemed unlikely. This was the year after their undefeated national championship season, and I was young enough to think that there was some connection between me being in love with the team and their national championship. I was yet to experience the unrequited love of a failing team.

Alabama was 8-2, but the big news was that Bear Bryant had suspended Joe Namath for drinking and replaced him with Steve Sloan, who had played mostly as a defensive back. With Namath out, no one, at least in our world, thought Alabama had a chance. It had been billed as the Battle of the South, and despite not having Namath, Bear Bryant had not tried to downplay the stakes of the game, telling reporters, "I wouldn't be surprised if it's not the best football game in the nation."

With a wet field, snow pushed to the side, it started badly for Ole Miss, and they settled into a war of attrition. On their second drive, Alabama kicked a field goal, then followed with another field goal after Ole Miss fumbled. "All we need is one good drive," my dad said, settling into his long coat. "They held 'em to three. Just need a solid drive."

But Ole Miss fumbled again in the wet, sloppy conditions, and Alabama got another field goal. "We just can't get out of our own way," Dad said, shaking his head.

"We've got Weatherly," I said, looking to be convinced.

"That's right. We've got Jimbo. We'll be okay." He unbuttoned a few buttons on his long coat and threw it over my legs. "That better?" I had been shivering. Weatherly was Jim Weatherly, the Ole Miss star quarterback. Namath got the national press, but Weatherly was tall and good-looking and had a quiet cool that inspired confidence. He played in a rock-and-roll band. Later he would go on to a career as a singer and songwriter, writing "Midnight Train to Georgia" among many hits. But for now, he was just the second-best and second-coolest quarterback in the SEC, not a bad distinction when Joe Namath was number one.

But Jimbo Weatherly was having an off game. The cold seemed to bother him. He threw an interception that led to another Alabama field goal. Nothing was clicking with the Ole Miss offense; one fumble led to another, and by the end of the game they had fumbled eleven times, an unimaginably high number for any team but especially one coached by Johnny Vaught, who always stressed fundamentals.

"Can't catch a break," my dad said. "Rebels just can't catch a break." I wasn't sure exactly what that meant, but it didn't sound good. Even when Ole Miss finally got a first down on the Alabama two-yard line, they still couldn't score. At the end, it was Alabama 12, Ole Miss 7. The Alabama student newspaper called it "the most important win of the Bear Bryant era." All I knew was that the Rebels had lost the Big One. The scene was ugly leaving the stadium. A good portion of the 83,000 had woken up hungover and pumped themselves up for the game with Bloody Marys and other toddies, sustained through the game with smuggled flasks. Now the Alabama fans were still drinking in celebration, and the Ole Miss faithful, those who had a drop or two left, were drinking to console themselves.

We shuffled down the crowded ramp of the old stadium surrounded by the sullen crowd. I had been crying, and my face was bright red from the tears and the cold. My father had his arm around me, and he was talking about next season.

"They'll be back next season. Better than this season. Jimbo Weatherly will be quarterback. They'll be back."

In the far corner of the parking lot, a cluster of Alabama fans taunted with choruses of "Hotty Toddy." One of the Ole Miss fans ran into the group, fists flying.

Dad steered us away. "They'll be better next year. You hungry? I'm hungry. You know somebody has to lose a game," he said. "It's easy if you win all the time. When you lose, it's harder. That's when fans have to stick with their team. We still love the Rebels, right?"

I nodded. Of course we did.

"That's because we love them even if they lose. Things aren't always easy. It's hard to lose, but it's a test."

"A test?"

"If you really love a team, you still love them. And if you are on a team and it loses, that's when you have to stick together. That's important. Just work harder and come back next time."

But Ole Miss never made it to another bowl game undefeated and never won another national championship.

LSU played Ole Miss at Oxford this year, a not small advantage given the insanity of Tiger Stadium. The morning of the game, I got up early and went for a run from the campus into Oxford. It was always a little startling to see the Grove filled with the red tents of game day. The green open space of the day before was transformed into a tent city, like an overnight refugee camp for partiers.

The university kept all tents out of the Grove until 9:00 p.m. the night before, and then there was a land rush to claim your space and set up tents. There was an odd etiquette that mostly allowed for groups to return to the same space year after year, though there was always some grumbling that every year it was harder than ever to get the right spot. This was no doubt true because the Grove scene seemed to grow more popular and there was only so much space.

I passed a couple in their late twenties slowly pulling a large red ice chest to their tent. He had a cup of coffee, and she had a glass of white wine. They each pulled on the chest and took turns with the drinks: one sip of coffee each, then a sip of wine. She waved her wineglass at me as I passed. "It's not as bad as it looks," she said, laughing. "I recommend the combination highly."

Downtown, I circled the deserted courthouse square of Oxford. My mother had spent her first night in Oxford, fresh off the train that doesn't run anymore, in a hotel right on the square. She had arrived a day earlier than expected and hadn't been able to get in touch with the university sorority officials who were planning to meet her. She had tried to get a glass of wine at the hotel restaurant, and that's when she learned for the first time that Oxford was dry. Now bars, restaurants, bookstores, and art galleries had transformed the town. *Smithsonian* magazine had named it one of the twenty best small towns in America. For years, the owner of Square Books, Richard Howorth, had served as mayor. There was something irresistible about a town that elected a bookstore owner mayor.

When I got back on campus, my father was walking along Circle Drive around the Grove. "What are you doing up this early?" I asked. He was wearing a ski jacket and scarf and looked almost rakish.

"We used to park out here," he said, waving at the Grove. "Back then, you could park here before games. That was real tailgaiting."

"Y'all want some coffee?" a woman asked. She was middle-aged and elegantly put together in a red dress and heels. It was a sophisticated look for this early—even for the Grove, where dressing up was something of a competitive sport among some. She had a coffeemaker plugged in on the table. "How about a sweet roll?"

We told her we'd love some. "You're out early," I said, diving into maybe the best sweet roll I'd ever tasted.

"My daughter's sorority is having a brunch. But it was our turn to set everything up at the tent. There're five of us, five couples, and we divide who sets up for each game. We've been doing this since we graduated. I guess that tells you how old I am."

"I'm ninety-five," my dad said.

"Good God!" she said. "That's amazing."

I was getting used to that shocked reaction to my father's age. I wasn't sure if it was that people thought he was younger or it was more the idea that anyone could be ninety-five. Whatever the cause, he seemed to enjoy the shock.

"I never in all my life thought I'd be this dressed up this early on a Saturday. Normally, I'd be out here in my sweats. But I just don't want to embarrass my daughter, you know?"

"You look great," Dad said.

"You get another sweet roll for that," she said, holding out a plate. I had the feeling that's what he had been hoping would happen.

We walked off licking our fingers. "You know," I said, "if you don't do campaigns, fall can be kind of nice." I gestured out at the Grove. "I've been running around doing campaigns like they were the most important thing in the world, while people were still coming to the Grove, enjoying life."

"Some people like that," Dad said.

"What?" I asked.

"Enjoying life," he said, with a smile. "But you enjoy campaigns, don't you?"

"I enjoy winning. No," I said, correcting myself, "I enjoy not losing. I realized a long time ago that it hurts more to lose than it feels good to win."

"Can you imagine not doing campaigns?" he asked.

"Today I could. Especially if Ole Miss wins." We sat down on a bench overlooking the Grove. A couple of students were trying to hang a crystal chandelier inside a tent.

"I'm not sure they've done that before," my father said.

"I'll tell you what I always liked most about campaigns. It's definite. You win or lose. You don't have to wonder if you did a good job. It must be like that with lawsuits."

He shrugged. "You've heard me say it before. A lot of being a good lawyer is avoiding lawsuits."

"I wouldn't have been good at that. I would want to try every one, even if I lost. Just to fight and see if I could have won. But that's why I would make a lousy lawyer."

We watched as the chandelier almost came tumbling down, caught at the last minute by a middle-aged man passing by with a red cup in one hand. He held it up like a trophy to applause.

"Nice catch," Dad said.

"Why do you think somebody wants a chandelier in a tent anyway?" I asked.

"To make it special," he said. "All these tents out here, but these folks will have a chandelier. I bet they do it for every night game. Their friends think it's funny, and they joke about it all year. It's why people have parties."

"To have fun?"

"To give themselves something to remember a special event. Memory works like that. You get older, you learn a lot about memory." He paused with a bittersweet look. "Good and bad. You know what I worry about you?" he asked, and before I could answer, he said, "You're too hard on yourself. You blame yourself too much if anything goes wrong in one of your campaigns. And"—he held up a big hand as I was starting to respond— "you've let work consume you too much. It's what you care most about now."

He was right, and I knew there was no point in arguing. "When you think about what made you the happiest, what was it?"

"Happiest? It was always family." He paused. "But you know that. You, your sister, your mother."

I nodded. It wasn't an unexpected answer, but there seemed to be no hesitation and not a hint of doubt. "And when you think about everything you've done, what makes you the most proud?"

He looked at me, surprised. "Proud? Tried to avoid that."

I was instantly thrown back into the years of Sunday school, the countless lessons of the foolishness of pride. Pride cometh before the fall. Be not proud. "Bad way to put it," I said, retreating. "What do you think of as your greatest achievement?"

He didn't say anything for a while, then got up and stretched, then sat back down. The sun was hitting the bench and warming up. It was a nice spot.

He put his arm on my shoulder. "You are. And your sister." I looked at him for a moment, then hugged him awkwardly, the two of us side by side.

"Love you," I said.

"Love you."

The LSU–Ole Miss game was one of those special gatherings of the clans of the football faithful. I ran into Curtis Wilkie, the former *Boston Globe* political reporter who was now teaching at the Ole Miss journalism school, as he was hurrying through errands on the Oxford square. "Everybody's in town," he said. "I don't think I've eaten a meal at home all week."

One of my favorite Louisiana cousins, Stuart Oliphant, drove all the way from Texas for the game. He had grown up going to LSU games with his dad, a Methodist minister. We met at the Grove, where the mood of the Ole Miss fans was pleasantly fatalistic. It's not that we expected to lose but more that everyone seemed determined to enjoy the day despite the likelihood of impending pain.

Stuart had been in the stands when LSU fielded their first African American players in 1972. (Interestingly, that same year LSU elected its first African American student body president.)

"I remember sitting in the end zone of Tiger Stadium with all the drunks," he said as we watched the Ole Miss team come through the Grove in the ritual Walk of Champions. "I was just a kid. Daddy was there and my brother. The first black LSU players, Lora Hinton and Mike Williams, came out on the field. I'd never heard cussing like that. I think it was the first time I heard the *n*-word.

"People were throwing these little empty bottles of booze out on the field, yelling. Then Hinton intercepted a pass, and everybody is standing up yelling for him. 'That Puerto Rican can play! Look at that Puerto Rican sum-bitch.'"

We laughed and watched the crowd mobbing the Ole Miss players. The crew-cut, all-white team of 1962 was now replaced by big strong kids who looked a lot like modern Mississippi: long hair, short hair, scruffy beards and locks. With Coach Hugh Freeze in an elegant suit and sunglasses, the team glided through the Grove's dappled sunlight.

"You guys," I said to Stuart, meaning LSU fans, "are going to leave here so happy. Ole Miss can hardly field eleven guys on defense."

"Maybe. But you know what worries me?"

"The long drive home tomorrow?"

"For these guys," he said, pointing to the end of the line of Ole Miss players disappearing through the crowd, "it's the biggest game of the year. Our guys are looking to Alabama."

"We already lost to Alabama," I moaned. "It was a slaughter."

"We'll see. I just have a bad feeling."

———

With the first Ole Miss interception, it started to feel as if something special might just happen. It was late in the first quarter, and LSU had shown why they were ranked number six in the country. They had phenomenal athletes who played with confidence and grace, including a receiver, Odell Beckham, who casually caught passes with one hand in the pregame warm-up. LSU was headed for what seemed like a certain score when a freshman Ole Miss defensive back flashed across the field to steal the ball from a surprised Beckham.

My father leaped to his feet, I next to him, and in that moment it was as if the years had shed away as effortlessly as tossing aside a quilt when getting out of bed in the morning. He was no different from the students below us, screaming in utter joy. This simple game had cut through our differences and our years with a powerful grace.

The interception was only one play, early in a long game, but it was enough to let you believe that tonight had a shot to be one of those magical games when luck and chance had decided to bless our side, if only for a few hours. Of course there was the equal possibility it was all a great tease, that our hopes had been raised, only to be dashed more brutally. But when you are playing one of the best teams in the country, you don't let a piece of hope drift by, convinced another, larger one will soon follow. And at the half, miraculously, Ole Miss led 10–0.

Everyone seemed more nervous at halftime than before the game. Then there had been a grudging anticipation of pain masked by the dark humor of those who expected to lose but still found a way to have fun. But now the door had been cracked open to the bright and happy land called upset. Everyone spoke quietly, respectfully, as if concerned about angering the gods of football through sins of pride.

We ate hot dogs and talked in subdued tones about how the crippled Ole Miss defense was playing with such heart. "They're not afraid," my dad said. "That's the key. They're playing like they're angry, not afraid."

When the second half began, I slumped down next to my father, preparing myself for the disaster sure to unfold. We'd had our fun, but the house always demands its payment, and in this case the number six team in the nation was surely the house. "I've got a bad feeling," I said to my father as Ole Miss kicked off.

"The Rebels want this more," my father said. "If it's close in the end, I think we'll take it."

To my amazement, the second half began well. Ole Miss scored on their first possession, making it 17–0. They looked the way we had expected LSU to look, running powerfully behind a dominating offensive line. "Can we leave now?" I said. "I know there's pain coming. I don't want the pain. I reject the pain."

And it came. On the kickoff, LSU's dazzling Odell Beckham ran through most of the Ole Miss team, until one desperate tackle brought him down on the thirty-nine-yard line. Half a dozen plays later, LSU scored. Ole Miss 17, LSU 7.

When Ole Miss got the ball, they promptly fumbled. "What did I tell you?" I moaned to my father.

He shrugged. "They just need to stop 'em now."

I'd heard this same reassurance from my dad since we first started going to games whenever it was time for the Rebels to make a stand. I'd found comfort in it, and because more often than not the Rebels did stop them, it inspired a deep faith in my father's power to will a commanding defensive stand. I wondered if, fifty years from now, fathers and sons would be sitting in the stands watching their favorite team and telling each other, "We just need to stop 'em now." I found that idea strangely reassuring, as if we were part of some timeless communion of sports.

For two plays, the Ole Miss defense was perfect, almost sacking the LSU quarterback twice, forcing two incomplete passes Then on a third and ten, he was chased by the defense but threw a beautiful pass for thirty-four yards. A huge groan rumbled through the stadium. Two plays later, LSU scored, and it was Ole Miss 17, LSU 14.

Ole Miss came back to score, and my father slapped my knee and sprang to his feet with the crowd. "We can beat these guys," he said. "We can do it."

With three minutes left in the game, it was tied, 24–24. Probably every Ole Miss fan was thinking about last week's game against Texas A&M, when the team fought ferociously only to lose in the last seconds. "Have faith," my father said. "Have faith."

The rest of the game wasn't pretty and hardly looked like destiny, but somehow Ole Miss ended up where Texas A&M had been the previous week. There were six seconds left in the game when the field goal team came out. The kicker had missed one earlier, and at forty-four yards out this kick was at the limit of his range. LSU fielded its biggest, tallest players, tremendous athletes with great vertical jump and pure fury in their hearts.

They were desperate to win a national championship. They had worked for years for it. Now this one skinny kid was trying to take that away.

And so he did. In the kick of his life, Andrew Ritter nailed it.

Then my father lifted me up in his arms in a great big bear hug, and this, I knew, was what I had missed most of all.

7

· · · ·

After the LSU game, I drove my parents down to New Orleans
for a few days. It was a drive that should take about five hours,
so naturally it took us most of the day. We drove south on Interstate 55, the main north-south route that divides Mississippi.
In disasters like Katrina, it became a primary escape route for
everyone leaving for safer ground. But for generations of Mississippians, I-55 and the older northbound highways of Mississippi had always been escape routes to a different life.

This was the route of the great exodus to the North that so
many African Americans took trying to find better jobs and
a better life. It was the road that a Mississippi governor, Kirk
Fordice, was driving on his way back from seeing his high school
girlfriend when he crashed and almost died. It was awkward that
his wife was living in the Governor's Mansion at the time, but
this was the way of Mississippi: you went north to Memphis or
south to New Orleans to escape, if only for a night or weekend.
In high school, my sister and I had come up with a friend to see
Jimi Hendrix play in Memphis one January. On the way back,
the electric windows of his parents' fancy car mysteriously lowered and refused to rise. It was about ten degrees, and we drove
the entire way with the heater on full, shivering, playing Hendrix
on an eight track. It was sublime.

Jackson is about halfway between Oxford and New Orleans. When we got to the outskirts of Jackson, my dad tapped me on the shoulder and gestured to his right. "Doesn't look like a good day," he said. I looked over, confused. Then I saw it. We were passing the building that housed his old law firm with the name of the firm on the outside. For an old-school lawyer like my dad, this hinted at advertising, and he loved to tease them that it probably flashed on and off when they won a big case.

"Not flashing," I said.

He nodded, smiling.

The law offices were in a prosperous business/shopping center development with a gleaming new Apple Store. Just a few miles away was the campus of St. Andrew's day school. It was the new incarnation of the rattrap mansion on North State Street where I had gone to elementary school. This was the "New Jackson," and if you had grown up here as I did, you would appreciate that "new" was truly better.

Jackson was more like the rest of the country now, with its chain stores and flurry of rush-hour traffic, but the loss of that individuality that came with the isolationism of earlier years was not to be grieved. For Mississippi, joining the mainstream was mostly progress. Jackson had a world-class bookstore, Lemuria, hosted the USA International Ballet Competition, had a newspaper that wasn't trying to turn back the clock, had better schools, public and private. A new civil rights museum was being built, helped by a large contribution from my father's law firm. There were still tremendous problems of poverty and race that seemed to improve with glacial slowness, but the efforts to seal it off from the rest of the country had ended.

I hadn't planned to, but I found myself turning off the interstate, drawn to our old neighborhood. My parents smiled and didn't object.

We passed Riverside Park, where I had learned to swim. When you grow up in a place with the long summers of Jackson, the delight of days in a pool is near primal. Riverside had been one of a handful of public pools sprinkled across Jackson, like an oasis in a desert. It was close to our house, and I could still remember the sense of joyful freedom when I first rode my bike from our house on Piedmont Street up the big hill to the pool. I was afraid my parents would say no, so I did the only natural thing and didn't ask permission. When I started out, I didn't tell myself I was going to ride all the way to the pool. I went to the end of Piedmont Street, which was the normal bike boundary my parents had established. Then I snuck a right on Riverside and just kept going. All the way there I expected a car to pull up alongside and some adult—my mother or father or a neighbor—to roll down the window, letting a gust of cool air from the clunky car air conditioner blow out, and say, "What in the world do you think you are doing?"

But that never happened. I kept riding until I got to the pool. Years later, I read this description of OPEC's founding: "They doubled the price of crude and when they didn't hear jets, they doubled it again." That was sort of how I felt riding to the pool. If not stopped, I was going to go.

Later that afternoon, I snuck back down the hill, taking the backstreets through our Belhaven neighborhood to avoid being seen on busy Riverside Drive. My swim shorts were dry, or so I thought, and wearing them wasn't incriminating. I'd wear swim trunks all day, every day in the summer. We all did, looking for hoses to run through or any backyard plastic pool, the ones that seemed to last only a few days before they exploded. I was feeling very proud of myself when I was standing in the kitchen, eating some leftover ham biscuits from a party. Wonderful, salty Virginia ham with soft biscuits was a standard at every party, and when I taste those flavors today, I can hear the clink of glasses, the high laughter of women, piano.

"Stuart Stevens, you've been swimming." I turned around to see an impish grin on Elzoria's face. I had a mouthful of biscuit. "You rode that little bike of yours up to the pool, and you went s-w-i-m-m-i-n-g."

"How do you—"

"Don't you even try," she said, laughing. "How was the water? That Stuberfield boy go with you?"

"He was there already." That was Al Stuberfield, who lived down the street and was my best friend. "I love to swim," I said. "I'm fast too."

"Don't brag on yourself. Somebody is always better. Pride cometh before the fall."

"Yes, ma'am. But I beat everybody."

"And tomorrow somebody will beat you. Don't you forget it."

"Yes, ma'am. Do you like to swim, Elzoria?"

"Me? Me?" She laughed. "You put me in that water and I'll drop like a rock."

"You can't swim?" I asked. I didn't know anyone who couldn't swim.

"Not a lick."

"You should come tomorrow, and I'll teach you," I said. "It's fun."

She looked at me, cocking her head in a way she had as if wondering how the world got this way.

"Well, we'll talk about that sometime," she said.

"You'll like it," I promised, grabbing another biscuit. She snatched it from my hand and took a bite.

"Mmmm. These things make my mouth too happy. I'm gonna be fat as you." She pinched my stomach, and I buckled over, giggling.

"I'm not fat!"

She tickled me harder.

Today there isn't a swimming pool at Riverside Park. There's now a handsome museum of natural science at the park, but for years the pool I loved sat empty, unused until finally it was filled in. Like all of the public pools across the state—and most of the South—the Jackson swimming pools were segregated. Though it didn't hit me until years later, that probably explained the odd look Elzoria gave me when I suggested I teach her to swim. When federal courts ordered that the Jackson pools be integrated, the city closed the pools rather than integrate. That prompted a challenge that went to the U.S. Supreme Court, and in 1971 the Court ruled 5-4 that Jackson closing its pools was consistent with the doctrine of separate but equal. If there were no open public pools, then blacks were not being singled out for discrimination. Everyone was being equally denied the right to swim through the five months of a Mississippi summer.

Madness? Of course. Once closed, the Jackson pools never reopened. In other towns across the state, they were either converted to private "clubs" for whites only or filled in. In the small town of Stonewall, named for Stonewall Jackson, in eastern

Mississippi, near Meridian, a beautiful Olympic-sized pool was filled with hundreds of dump truck loads of the red soil that had never been as productive as the Delta's more fecund black earth. Years later, a local businessman who had sweet memories of summers spent at the pool paid to have it dug out, rebuilt, and reopened for the public.

The public explanation for the closing of the Jackson pools was "closed for maintenance." Around that time, my parents decided to build a pool in our backyard. When the neighborhood was first being developed, my dad had bought a double lot that ran between Piedmont Street and Howard Street. Our house faced on the dead end Piedmont Street, and the backyard, where they built the pool, faced onto Howard Street. This allowed access to the pool from another street, away from the house. It felt not like a backyard private pool but more like a neighborhood pool, and so it was. Pretty much always, the pool was open to whoever wanted to use it.

We drove from Riverside Park through the old neighborhood, down Howard Street to the back of our old house. I hadn't been here in years. I parked the Toyota on Howard Street. The lot in back of our house where my parents had built the swimming pool was once again a backyard. The pool had disappeared.

"They filled it in," I said.

"So they did," my father said.

"I think I heard about this," my mother said.

Part of the old fence was still there, redbrick columns and cedar planking. I got out to stretch and look around. It was hot and very green, like a long, lush tunnel. This little corner of the world had meant a lot to me. Next door was the house where my aunt Dorothy had lived her entire adult life, and I had written my first articles and short stories in her basement. She was of the MacLaren clan with a fondness for all things Scottish and would bring down shortbread cookies for me to eat. Her husband, my father's older brother, had died young of a heart condition from rheumatic fever as a child. One door down was the little house where my grandmother lived. I had wandered in and out of her kitchen in my early years. She was always reading, everything from mysteries to Shakespeare. My father often made the case that the South was something of a hidden matriarchy, that the impact of so many men being lost in the Civil War had created a society dominated by strong women. It was an interesting theory, and women like my aunt Dorothy and my grandmother were good evidence.

When I was in junior high in Jackson at the school where my aunt taught most of her life, she had sat me down before the ninth grade for a "talk." It was in her small living room, dominated by blue carpet and paintings by my grandmother. She served strong black coffee and her Scottish shortbread. She always assumed I wanted coffee, which made me feel older. "This year Bailey will be integrated," she said. Bailey was Bailey Junior High, where she taught and I attended. She was more serious than usual. Normally, there was a teasing hint to her eyes.

"Yes, ma'am."

"It looks like there will be one black male student in your grade and one black female. I think there should be more, but I don't think there will be."

"Yes, ma'am." I didn't know what to say.

"I want you to think about what it would be like to leave Bailey and go across town to Peeples," a black junior high school in south Jackson. "You wouldn't know anybody or have any friends. You remember what it was like when you started at St. Andrew's and didn't know anyone? You were really nervous."

"I was?"

She laughed. "For a day or two. But St. Andrew's was small, and the kids were all a lot like you. Imagine going to a big school where you didn't know anyone." Bailey had more than five hundred students. "And imagine if you were one of two white students."

I didn't say anything.

"The student's name is Sammy Edwards. I want you to do everything you can to help Sammy."

"What's he like?"

She thought for a minute. "I don't really know. I've read his record. He's a smart fellow."

"Does he play sports?"

"He did, but I'm not sure he will at Bailey."

"Why not?"

She hesitated. "It might be hard being the only black player on a team."

I nodded.

"I want you to help Sammy."

"Help him?"

"He's going to sit next to you in the classes you have. Mrs. Hester and I arranged that." Mrs. Hester was her closest friend, another formidable woman who had taught at the school forever.

"Okay."

"And just . . . help him. You get along with everybody. Make it easier on him."

"He may not like me."

She reached out and took my hand. "This is important."

"Yes, ma'am." I tried to think of what to say or ask but had no idea. But then something came to me. "He's not a little guy, is he?"

She knew what I meant. If he was small, it would make it easier for him to be picked on. "No," she said. "He's tall for his age. And he's brave, or he wouldn't be doing this."

"Nobody made him?"

She shook her head. "It was his choice. All the children coming to the schools being integrated made the choice."

"Takes guts," I said and meant it.

"I've talked to the principal. You won't get into trouble standing up for Sammy."

"You mean, if there was trouble and—"

She nodded. "I think he'll understand."

Now I was nervous. The idea of spending the school year getting into fights for somebody else sounded lousy, even if I wouldn't get into trouble.

"I know you'll help him," she said.

I tried and I'd like to think I helped, but I don't think I did. I sat next to Sammy, who was tall and quiet. He was a good student who always had his homework done on time, which not many of us did, at least with his regularity. But if he needed a friend, and surely he must have, I failed spectacularly. In some *To Kill a Mockingbird* fantasy, we would have found a way to become friends, discovering we had more in common than we realized, maybe a love of cars or maybe girls or football. That never happened. All year I sat next to him, but there was such a gulf between us, there was no use pretending. He knew it from the start, certainly wiser if not older than I. He had steeled himself for this experience, and who was I to say that was wrong? I sat next to him a few times at lunch, and we tried to make conversation. But it was all so transparently phony. It was as though he wanted to put down his fork, stop eating the daily mystery meat, and say, "Look, I know what you are trying to do. That's fine, but I don't need your help and don't want to be friends with somebody who thinks they are helping me just by being my friend. I have friends. They just aren't at this school. You have friends. We don't need to be friends so you can feel better and tell yourself you helped me."

Or so I imagined. After the first couple of weeks, I quit seeing Sammy at lunch. I suppose he just skipped. All that year, I sat next to him in class, both of us in our different worlds. I'm sure he must have been brushed in the halls, heard whispered taunts, found notes in his locker. But he had a quiet dignity about him that seemed above all of that.

My aunt would ask me from time to time how I thought he was doing. I always said fine, great, but of course I had no idea. "Have you invited him home after school?" she asked one weekend, when I was hanging out at her house, watching television and eating her shortbread.

I felt a quick rush of shame. The thought had never occurred to me. But then I didn't ever really invite anybody over, like some "playdate" of kids. There were sports and then my pals in the neighborhood; we were in and out of one another's houses all the time. Friends just showed up.

But one day I waited until the end of a social studies class when everybody was filing out. Sammy and I sat in the far-left row, the one nearest to the windows and farthest from the door, and we were usually the last to leave.

"Hey, Sammy," I said, "wait up." He turned and looked at me with a friendly look.

"Yep?"

"I was wondering, uh, if you wanted to come over sometime, when school is out."

"Come over?" He seemed genuinely confused.

"To my house."

He frowned. "Why? Is this a school thing?"

"Nah, nothing like that. I just thought it might be fun."

"Yeah, sure. I got that." He nodded. "That's nice."

"We could go swimming?"

"Yeah."

Then I was suddenly embarrassed. What a stupid thing to say.

"You got a pool?" he asked.

"Yeah," then I quickly added, "it's like a neighborhood thing."

"So we'd swim with your neighbors?" He smiled. "Man. You talk to them?"

"No, but I mean, it's our pool."

He nodded. "That's really nice of ya. But I help my mom out taking care of my younger sister after school."

"Right. Yeah. Well, look, anytime you want to, we should do it."

"That would be real nice."

"Okay, great," I said. "Talk to you."

Of course it never happened. I mentioned it once or twice again, and Sammy always said the same thing: "That would be nice."

When I told my aunt, she nodded and said, "It's good you asked. That's all that matters."

The next year, I went away to a boarding school in Alexandria, Virginia, which had yet to integrate. I was in study hall when it was announced that Martin Luther King Jr. had been shot. Some students applauded. But others stared silently into space, and a few cried. Soon we watched the orange glow of Washington, D.C., in flames from behind the walls of the school.

That was a different era. Jackson now had an African American mayor. I got back in the car. The three of us—me, my mother, and my father—sat there in their old Toyota, not saying anything, but thinking about the past, each lost in different memories.

"Do you remember," I asked my mother, "when you started bringing all those pregnant teenagers to the house?"

"I can't believe you remember that," she said.

"Remember? How could I forget hugely pregnant teenage girls in bathing suits?"

It was the first time I'd seen pregnant women, at least in bathing suits, much less teenage pregnant women, and the first time I'd seen black women with white women hanging out together. It was during a period when my mother was volunteering with a "maternity home" that helped young mothers, mostly unmarried, during and after pregnancies. Most were teens whose families either couldn't support them or didn't want to.

"You told me that it was why I should study really hard and do well in school."

"I did not," she said, laughing.

"You did. And I think I was probably in grad school before I realized if I got a lousy grade, I wouldn't get pregnant."

Ostensibly, the reason my parents built a pool was the serious problems my father was having with his back. My mother had read somewhere that JFK had helped his bad back with swimming and thought it might help my father. At least that's what they told everybody at the time. Now I understood there were other reasons. It was a small statement against the insanity of Jackson's closing public pools.

"If they had kept the pools open, would we have built a pool?" I asked.

"It was good for your father's back," my mother said. She was in the front seat. My dad was in the back.

"It made a big difference for me," Dad said. "Really helped my back."

"The way I figure it," I said, sort of joking, "we had one of the first integrated pools in Jackson."

A look of real sadness flashed over my mother's face. "To close those pools so nobody could use them. Jackasses."

I hadn't thought about our old pool for years, but there was something that bothered me about its disappearance. It had been a place where so many hot afternoons and evenings had passed, endless games of Marco Polo with the neighborhood. The pregnant teenagers wouldn't have come to the house if it hadn't been for the pool.

It was at that pool that I remember feeling like something close to an adult for the first time. It was when I was home from boarding school, the spring of 1968. Somehow my mother had invited a bunch of college kids who were working for the Eugene

McCarthy campaign to stay at the house. They were trying to organize delegates to the Democratic convention to commit to McCarthy in anticipation of a contested convention. My mother was a great collector of people, and when I got home for spring vacation and there was this group of college students sleeping in the basement and around the house, it didn't seem odd.

Though they were only college students—all from Ivy League schools—they seemed much older, very cool, and the two women were beautiful. They listened to Peter, Paul, and Mary and seemed to be having a great time in Mississippi, even though they knew their candidate was headed to defeat.

They disappeared early and came back late and would sit out by the pool, drinking beer and smoking cigarettes and talking. I was out by the pool cleaning up one evening when they came out for a swim. I started to leave, but they asked me to stay and talk. To my astonishment, they seemed interested in what I thought, what I thought about Mississippi and whether it was changing. Did I think the race "situation"—that's how a lot of people called things then, a "situation"—was getting better or worse? Did I think the war in Vietnam was winnable? It wasn't as if they were just being nice to me; they seemed genuinely interested in what I had to say, which was completely unimaginable. It was like a peek into another, exciting world, of what life might become.

Now I understood the world better, and there was something about that pool being filled in that made me feel suddenly old. We got back in the car and drove to New Orleans.

8

My parents spent half the year in a funny old apartment building on St. Charles Avenue in New Orleans. The apartment was on the edge of the Garden District, across the street from the Pontchartrain hotel, where childhood visits for its famous "mile-high pie" were a big deal. It was a stacked combination of vanilla, strawberry, chocolate, and peppermint ice cream topped with meringue. I would look forward to that for days. My mother liked the apartment building because it was familiar, a place where parents of her friends had gravitated when they moved out of their family homes. It had history and context that help stave off the chaos of a changing world. It wasn't a fancy building, but the comfort they sought wasn't in the gimmicks real estate agents now love to market, the granite countertops or bathrooms big enough for a party. They found the building had a soothing continuity. There were people who had worked there for decades, even some second-generation employees. Within a couple of weeks of moving in, my parents were best friends with everyone who worked in the building. This was their way.

It was the idea that things didn't change much in New Orleans that was its greatest appeal to so many but also its greatest curse. Once New Orleans had been the South's most dynamic, innovative, evolving urban center, but somewhere that had stopped, and it had become a theme park. A couple of centuries of focus on creativity and vivacity had shifted to an obsession with "preservation." Everybody talked about the problems of New Orleans, if only because they were impossible to ignore—the institutionalized corruption, the crime, the poverty—but always the solutions were about "restoring" New Orleans, the assumption that the answers lay in a greater appreciation of the past than an embrace of the future. It was as if New Orleans had chosen Miss Havisham's room as the model home of the future.

Like almost everyone who encounters New Orleans, I had gone through a period of enchantment, had roamed through the clubs, greeted many dawns over beignets at the French Market, read *A Confederacy of Dunces* like it was some sacred text. I'd gone along with the glib assumptions about the city—the food was great, the culture rich—and my only defense can be that I never really believed it.

It was as if New Orleans had conducted an experiment of what the outcome would be if a society placed the greatest value on eating and drinking and made hard work a social negative. It wasn't the poor African Americans of the Ninth Ward who didn't like to work; it was the rich white people. At uptown New Orleans dinner parties, it was more socially acceptable to admit to loving McDonald's than confessing how much you enjoyed working. Before Katrina, New Orleans had faced a catastrophic disaster for over a century. In Holland, they built locks and dams. In New Orleans, they got drunk and threw beads at each other. My mother never liked it when I went off on New Orleans, and truth was, I still had a soft spot for it, maybe the way the

French loved Jerry Lewis; it didn't make sense, but there was still a little pleasurable tingle.

But mostly the point of living in New Orleans was to escape being exposed to the need to do anything new and to still feel good about that, even superior. That's why I almost fell out of my chair when my father said, "I want us to do something we've never done before." We were having breakfast in their apartment. Across Canal Street, just down from the Pontchartrain hotel, a couple of bars had stayed open late into the night, and I'd slept poorly, waking up to shouts of the drunken hilarity. Rampaging crowds of drunks were to New Orleans what rain was to Seattle, more noticeable in the absence.

"Never done before?" I asked. "In New Orleans?" I'd been coming to New Orleans since that first Sugar Bowl a whole bunch of years earlier. There wasn't anything new to do. At least I didn't think so.

"The World War II museum," my father said. "You haven't been yet, have you?"

"No." I liked the way he included "yet," as if it were inevitable, just a matter of time.

"We'll fix that," he said.

"Thank you for your service," the forty-something man said, shaking my father's hand.

My father nodded, the way he did when he was slightly embarrassed. Then the man hugged him. My father looked over his shoulder and raised his eyebrows. Off to the side, a British couple in their twenties with a young son stood by with an iPhone, waiting to take a photograph with my dad.

This was happening because my dad was a World War II vet and the museum gives vets a large hangtag to wear, like a credential. It was done up nicely in red, white, and blue and said in large, block letters, simply, WORLD WAR II VETERAN. My dad slipped it around his neck as his entry pass into the museum. He wasn't expecting it to attract a lot of attention.

"You were in the South Pacific?" the Englishwoman asked, after I took a photograph of her and her husband and young son posing by my father. In the background was a Pearl Harbor exhibit.

"Yes," he said, still a little taken aback by the attention.

"Were you over there very long?" her husband asked.

"I spent twenty-eight months on ship without a night ashore," he said. "But a lot of others had it much worse. They had to stay onshore." It was sort of a joke, but the couple seemed too startled to get it.

"Where were you?" the man asked.

A small group had gathered around my dad. He hesitated for a moment, then said, "I'll show you." He turned and took a few steps to a map of the South Pacific island.

"I had orders to report to LST Flotilla 7 somewhere in the South Pacific. No one knew exactly where it was. I started in San Francisco. An aircraft carrier dumped me on the northern shore of Australia, and then I got a ride on a passenger ship the Australian navy had commandeered over to New Guinea. They let me out on a beach, and I was greeted by fierce-looking New Guinea natives whose only English was the worst kind of profanity imaginable that the Australians had taught them. I'd come halfway around the world to hear curses I'd never imagined."

He traced the journey on the map, smiling slightly at the

memory. "They took me to some Australians and Americans there, and nobody had heard of Flotilla 7, but they told me to keep going up the coast. So I got another ride and eventually found LST Flotilla 7." He was doing what so many veterans did when they talked about the war, focusing on the absurdity of it and grabbing the bits of humor.

"I'm sorry, sir," the Englishwoman asked, "but what is an LST?"

This had taken on the feel of an impromptu lecture, and the volunteer guides of the museum drew closer. This entire wing was dedicated to the South Pacific, arranged in chronological order. "We called them Large, Slow Targets," my father said. "But their real names were Landing Ships, Tanks. They were longer than the length of a football field and used to land troops ashore. That's what we did. We went from island to island."

"How many landings did you participate in?" I asked quietly.

He paused for a minute, pulling the number up. "Twenty-eight. Twenty-eight different invasions."

There was a long silence while the number sank in. Finally, the Englishwoman hugged him.

Later we ate in the museum café that had a 1940s theme. We were both tired. I think I was more emotionally exhausted. "Did you see that display with the estimates of the American casualties of a Japanese invasion?" I asked. "Half a million to over a million U.S. dead or wounded. The army had produced over half a million Purple Hearts."

"We were headed to Okinawa to prepare for the invasion. That's when they dropped the first of those awful bombs." He looked away, but I could see him tear up. "Then they dropped the second awful bomb." "Awful bomb": it was a description I'd never heard him use before. In its very ordinariness, it suddenly made the reality of massive death more personal and specific.

"When we got to Okinawa, instead of loading combat troops, which had been our original mission, after the surrender we loaded with equipment for a weather station," Dad said. "We sailed off the northern tip of Japan. We were about a hundred yards offshore, and a boat paddled out with old Japanese men. We didn't have anybody who spoke Japanese, and they didn't speak a word of English. But we knew they had been suffering. They were skin and bones. So we gave them a boat filled with food for their village."

He smiled. "They were so grateful." We sat quietly and ate our sandwiches. When we were finished, Dad looked around as if noticing the café for the first time. "They did a really nice job with this. Yes, sir, they did." Then, as we started to get up, he said, "I often thought about how if the war had gone on, those Japanese who came out to our ship for help would have been terrified of us. And heaven knows what might have happened to them."

Back at the apartment, I asked him if he remembered much about the different landings or if they all blurred together. My mother was out running errands, and it was just the two of us in the smallish apartment. It was good for her to get out without having to worry about him.

"I don't think about it much," he said. "But that fellow from the museum asked me the same question when he came." The World War II museum had an extensive oral history project, and a young historian had traveled to Asheville to interview him a few years earlier.

"So I got to thinking about it and made a list."

"A list?"

"Of the landings." He went into the bedroom and came back with two pages. "I think this was everything."

I read through it. It was a list of twenty-eight landings he had participated in, with some brief notes on each: "frequent air attacks," "heavy air (kamikaze), mortar, artillery fire, severe casualties, ships and personnel," "four LST's severely damaged," "midget sub, air and mortar fire."

I sat back and tried to imagine what it was like: the kamikaze planes coming in waves, the screams of the wounded and dying, seeing other ships go down and wondering if you were next. I remembered him telling me about a kamikaze pilot barely missing the ship and being so close that for an instant he could lock eyes with the pilot in his death spiral.

"Which was the worst?" I asked and was immediately sorry I had. I was trying to bring order to the unimaginable. Rank the horrors, like an Internet listicle, and that would make it seem less terrifying. He looked at the list, lost in thought. Then he shook his head. He put the list down. "Let's talk about football. Who are we playing next weekend? Arkansas?"

"That's in two weeks. We've got Idaho this weekend. It's homecoming."

"Idaho?" He made it sound totally impossible, as if it were the University of Mars. I pretty much felt the same way.

"Yep. Idaho. Then Arkansas. Then Troy."

"Troy? Where is Troy?"

"Alabama. They can be good. Tough school. Not big, but tough."

"I hate games like that. We don't get any credit if we win, and it scares me to death."

"Yep. Then Missouri."

"Missouri? They're good this year."

"Really good. If we can beat them, we can get back in the top twenty, I bet."

"Where is it this year?"

"Starkville."

He grimaced. "That's a shame."

I nodded. It was comforting to walk through the rest of the year, a reassuring rosary of familiarity. The football schedule was everything that list of island landings was not. The twenty-eight landings were a chronicle of chaos and pain, but a season of weekends built around the rituals of football was dependable in its pleasures and the predictability and scale of its disappointments. Many people loved to point to the game as a metaphor for life, spinning out the lessons learned on the field to the landscape of life. There was surely truth in that, but it had never interested me much. The football that my father and I loved was too good to try to look for some usefulness in it any more than you'd go to church really expecting a limp to be healed. It was good because it was good, and that was enough.

This love of college football and its importance in life's scheme are natural for a southerner but difficult for the uninitiated to grasp. When I first moved to New York City in the 1980s, it was not a happy time in the city's fortunes. Subways resembled filthy, graffiti-covered prison cells. Everyone talked about crime the way Alaskans talk about bears or ski patrollers discuss avalanches. But I loved it. Like generations of expats in a foreign land, I fell into a crowd of fellow countrymen: southerners and mostly Mississippians. They were everywhere; it was years before I had any close friends in the city who weren't southern. In retrospect, that seems depressing, but it troubled me not at all in the moment. The crime, the postapocalyptic subways, the never-ending hunt for decent apartments that had perplexed every wave of New Yorkers since the Dutch, that all seemed part of the assumed rigors of big-city life. It was to be expected, and complaining would have been like paying lots of money for a trip to the rain forest and grousing it was wet. That was New York. It was how the city worked and people lived.

But every fall weekend, we would slide into a deep, predictable funk. We wanted to watch football—real football. At some point before each weekend, a depressing series of phone calls would commence among southern expats over the scarcity and quality of the football options on New York City television. "Holy Cross versus Harvard? Can you believe it? My high school played better football."

It was much as I imagine growing up in a culture with wonderful, distinctive food—India or the Szechuan Province of China—and moving to a drab place where the only options were awful strip mall restaurants that were all the more insulting for their claims to authenticity: "Real Indian" or "Genuine Chinese." They called these sad northeastern college efforts "football," but it was hardly a creature of the same species. Once a few of us dragged up to see Columbia play, and we left before the half. It wasn't just what was happening on the field; it was the entire experience. The few students who condescended to come seemed more interested in the mocking hipness of playing at being football fans. Some actually read books during the game. This was like bringing a six-pack to church to get through the sermon. "Like Communion served to atheists at the Joyce Kilmer rest stop on the New Jersey Turnpike," a friend described it as we rode back on the subway. Another friend was so depressed he flew home the next weekend for the Ole Miss–LSU game and never came back to New York. I didn't blame him a bit.

When there was a good game on television—and good meant that it had to involve a top southern, preferably SEC, team—we'd gather at one of our small apartments and stare at the screen, each of us homesick in a different way. It wasn't just that we missed going to the games; we missed being fans who could find comfort in the presence of other fans. When you showed up at an Ole Miss–Alabama game or an Auburn-Alabama game, life's complicated choices were reduced to a binary definition: you were for one team or the other, and whom you were for was pretty much all anyone needed to know. It was an identity that superseded all others.

Most of us had come to New York because we believed, on some level, that we had no choice. It was both a test of who we were and a way to define who we might become. It wasn't a fear of failure at home that drove us to New York but a fear that success at home might be all too satisfying. The expats in my crowd had no illusions about the South. We were scornful of those we deemed "professional southerners," those living in New York who tried to define themselves by some pretense that they came from a more genteel and cultured world.

But all of that changed on fall Saturdays, when we would gather in a self-congratulatory orgy of southern boosterism and shared loathing of the northeast brand of football. It gave us an opportunity to be smug, a joyful rarity for us in New York, but most of all it was an affirmation that though we may come from a not-so-perfect spot, we believed in something larger than ourselves that made us better than ourselves. In a confusing world, this festival of southern football was a constant that rarely disappointed.

One of the great virtues of the South is the assumption that football is important. When my parents and I were in New Orleans and saw old friends of theirs, no one thought it was odd that we were spending months going to Ole Miss games. It was hard to imagine a like reaction in Connecticut if you announced plans of taking three months off and going to every, say, Brown game. It would be seen, at best, as quirky, sort of like closely following jai alai or having strong opinions on who should play for the United States in the Croquet World Championship. But in the South, even in New Orleans, organizing a life around college football games seemed like a perfectly reasonable endeavor.

By Thursday before the next game, we all were eager to get back to Oxford. That was the rhythm of a fan's life, and I loved that it was now the focus of our lives. We drove to Oxford and settled back in the hotel on campus. My father and I immediately headed to the student union for the frozen yogurt we'd come to love. The union was filled with spirit signs of homecoming.

MASH THOSE IDAHO POTATOES! read a huge sign. My father shook his head with a pained expression. "Ole Miss is playing Idaho? Idaho?"

"It's strange," I agreed.

"If you coach for Idaho," my father asked, "what do you tell your players at halftime? Go play like potatoes?"

I laughed. "Their mascot is the Vandals."

"The Vandals?" He thought for a minute, then said, "I don't believe it."

I pulled up the University of Idaho Web site on my iPhone and read it to him: "Don't use your dictionary to find Idaho's definition of a Vandal. No, Idaho's student-athletes go by a name earned nearly a century ago by a basketball team coached by Hec Edmundson, whose teams played defense with such intensity and ferocity that sports writers said they 'vandalized' their opponents."

"They're named after a basketball team?" My father frowned. He and I both found basketball to be a slightly suspect sport.

"Apparently."

He looked pained. "What's their record this year?"

I pulled it up. "This is encouraging," I said. "They lost to the University of North Texas 6–40."

"Six to forty?" my father marveled. "Is University of North Texas any good?"

"Not that good. Then they lost to University of Wyoming 10–42."

"Good Lord."

"And Washington State 0–42."

"They have a good team. Washington State," my father said.

"Yep. And hey, they beat Temple 26–24. In Idaho. It was their homecoming."

"Nobody wants to lose homecoming. But Temple? From Philadelphia? I didn't know they played football. I thought it was a basketball school. So that's it? They win any other games this year?" my father asked.

I reviewed the results. "Nope. Lost to Fresno and Arkansas State too."

"This is definitely encouraging," he agreed. "Looks like a good homecoming match."

"Come on," I said to my dad. "I want to show you something."

We walked out of the student union and toward downtown. "Hear that?" I asked.

It was warm, more like August than November, one of those perfect days that are a reminder of how much summer will be missed. In the distance, a familiar song carried through the soft air. My father perked up, like a bird dog on a scent.

"Band practice," I explained.

We had walked to the edge of the campus and were in front of the band building. THE PRIDE OF THE SOUTH: OLE MISS BAND, the sign read. It was redbrick and formidable. Around the side was the practice field for the band. "This used to be the high school," my father said, "University High School. They had football games around back." I didn't know that, but it made sense. It looked like a high school, one of those imposing structures they built for schools when the formality of the buildings seemed connected to the seriousness of the educational task.

Behind the band building on the old high school's football field, the Ole Miss band, dressed in shorts and jeans, was practicing for homecoming. The band director conducted from a stepladder. He'd shout instructions to move this section here or that section over there, and a seemingly random group of students would transform into order. It resembled some large-scale game of chess with human pieces. They were practicing the "Ole Miss Alma Mater," a favorite at the games. It was lyrical and elegiac, a song from my youth. It was an odd song to play at a football game, sad and haunting, but this was Mississippi, and anything that could evoke a sense of loss was powerful medicine. I looked over at my dad, and he was smiling.

"Do you know what the lyrics are to it?" I asked.

He thought for a moment. "There are words? No one sings it. I don't have a clue."

I pulled up the words on my iPhone.

"Is everything in there?" he asked, nodding to my phone.

"All human knowledge," I assured him. "Found it. Here are the lyrics: 'Way down south in Mississippi, there's a spot that ever calls. Where amongst the hills enfolded, stand old Alma Mater's Halls.

"'Where the trees lift high their branches, to the whispering Southern breeze. There Ole Miss is calling, calling, to our hearts fond memories.'"

I looked up to find Dad frowning. "I think there's a reason nobody ever sings it," he said.

We watched as the student musicians joked around, looking bored, like a random collection of students who had been handed these odd things called instruments. But then, when the director's baton went up and they poised to play, something quite miraculous happened. They were transformed from just kids into some force transcendent. They became magicians conjuring miracles from the air.

In *Geronimo Rex,* Barry Hannah's brilliant first book, he described the powerful effect of a southern marching band: "The band was the best music I'd ever heard, bar none. They made you want to pick up a rifle and just get killed somewhere." So it was with the scruffy bunch who would form up on Saturdays in brilliant uniforms and transform themselves into the "Pride of the South" band. They tore into a medley that was a standard of every game. At the heart of it was the revised version of "Dixie" that the band now played.

Like every Ole Miss fan, I'd grown up with the Ole Miss band playing "Dixie," an assumed ritual like the singing of the national anthem. It was the Ole Miss football anthem. It was our anthem. Today it is popular for sports fans to call themselves "nation": "Red Sox Nation" or "Who Dat Nation" for the New Orleans Saints. But when "Dixie" played at Ole Miss games, it represented the lost glory of an actual nation. No one ever died for the right to form Red Sox Nation. Tens of thousands died for the brief existence of the Dixie nation.

In those days, the band would play "Dixie," Colonel Reb waved his sword, the Confederate flags would fly, and for that moment it could recapture a past as glorious as the last dance at Tara, when victory was assured and soon the Yankees would be taught a lesson. At the finale, the crowd would rise and join as one, shouting, "The South shall rise again!"

Inevitably, the irony, if nothing else, of having a team that was more than half African American charging to battle behind Colonel Reb and the Confederate battle flag became difficult to ignore. The school dropped Colonel Reb in 2003 and banned Confederate flags. That left "Dixie," which was a tougher call to ban. Though frequently assumed to have been a Confederate anthem, the song was actually a favorite of Abraham Lincoln, who had it played at the announcement of Robert E. Lee's surrender. But its fate as an Ole Miss regular was probably sealed with the crowd chant of "The South shall rise again" that rose up with the finale. It didn't help that the Ole Miss band wore uniforms modeled after Confederate battle dress. But the idea of Ole Miss football with no "Dixie," no Colonel Reb, and no Rebel flags was hard for many to grasp. As one Mississippi friend of mine, a former McGovern worker who now gave large sums to the Democratic Party, put it scornfully, "We might as well be the Syracuse of the South."

Instead of a complete ban on "Dixie," a compromise was reached. A modified version of "Dixie" would be allowed as part of a longer medley. Like the approaching death of a loved one, the final days of the original "Dixie"—"From Dixie with Love" was the full title—were marked with solemn ceremonies: the last playing at a special performance at the Grove in 2010. For the true believers, it was like the killing of the Latin Mass for a cheaper, junk-food variety more digestible to a broader audience.

Before my dad and I went to the season's first game at Vanderbilt, I realized that a part of me would want the games to be as they had always been. I remembered too well that simple joy when the cheerleaders would throw bundles of Confederate flags into the stands to be passed around like muskets at dawn reveille. Had somebody handed me a Confederate flag when the Rebels took the field, I'd have waved it out of pure muscle memory and maybe more. Or if that sweaty hot night in Nashville, Colonel Reb had made one more fateful, doomed charge through the goalpost chased by the band in their old-style Confederate uniforms playing the unrepentant "From Dixie with Love," I'd have stood and shouted, "The South shall rise again!" at the end with a clean heart. It would have been a piece of frozen time handed to me by a benevolent God, and I'd have licked it like an ice cream cone, joyous and grateful.

But I'd never be that young boy again, and while the tall man in the hat and the sport coat who would pick me up after every touchdown was still here, now he had his hand on my shoulder to keep a little steady. I knew the Rebel flags wouldn't wave again, and I'd never be swung through the air while rebel yells exploded all around us and the band broke into "Dixie." But listening to even that ersatz "Dixie" brought those moments back, how it felt jumping up on the wooden bleacher to be a little taller and hug my father and know then, without a doubt, that I was the luckiest kid on earth.

We stood watching the band work through the medley, moving smartly in formation now, as if the music demanded respect. They came to the "Dixie" section, and it wasn't quite the same as the old "Dixie," but by God it was awfully good. It was a song of loss, and that made it more real and stirring than an ode to victory. When I had heard the song as a child, I always assumed, probably like every other white southern son, that it was an ode to the southern way of life, that while we might have lost the battle called the Civil War, we had won that other war, that our values and our way of life had proven superior to the crasser, mercantile ways of the North.

But now I understood it wasn't about some hidden victory; it was just about loss. We lost. They won. It sounded sad because it was sad. It made you want to cry because loss was sad and defeat painful. The South was part of that brotherhood of cultures which learn to erect such beautiful homages to loss that it was easy to forget that they were still about loss and suffering. Surely this was their purpose. To be who I was when I was a boy was to be raised in a world that taught you it was right and essential that your people had been defeated but it was also right and essential to respect and mourn the loss. This, perhaps more than anything, defined what it was to be southern: to know the world celebrated your defeat, and to join in that celebration was required to be accepted into the company of civilized men and women. It is still living with the Civil War that separates the South from the North, more than victory or defeat. No one in the North thinks about the Civil War, which is the ultimate humiliation for the South. To win a war is to be free to move on. To be conquered is to live with the consequences forever. The descendants of Joshua Chamberlain are no doubt rightly proud of his actions turning back the charge that desperate day on Little Round Top, but are they haunted by it?

It was here at Ole Miss that the University Greys mustered up so they could meet their fate at Gettysburg, so eager and honored to lead Pickett's Charge into the slaughterhouse, attacking up the hill in daylight against fixed positions, dying and dying and dying until there were none left to die. It is in their honor the statue stands in the Grove.

The music faded, and the band director barked new instructions. Next to me, my father sighed. "You know, I'm tired," he said, and he looked it. Now that the rush of the music was passing, we were facing a long walk back.

"Should we call Mother to come get us?"

"Nope. Let's walk. Too nice outside."

It was a beautiful, warm afternoon, one of those days you want to frame and keep to pull out on the gray days to remember. We headed off as the band kicked into "Rebel March," the classic beats of a fight song. We both smiled. He put his arm around me, and we walked back through the campus.

Some might argue that it is a fluke of history that American homecoming is connected to football. Such people, of course, would be philistines and doubters and most likely Yankees.

Few Mississippians would think basketball or baseball worthy endeavors to organize an emotional reunion. And it's difficult to imagine anyone suggesting an American homecoming game would be the same if celebrated over soccer. Yes, of course, soccer is the world's most popular sport, "the beautiful game" that transcends cultures and languages. This is precisely why it is so unsuited to the unique rituals of American homecoming. Soccer is the UN of sports; a game that belongs to the world doesn't belong to anyone. You can't come "home" to a sport that isn't your home.

Like it or not, America has always been a violent country, and football is a domesticated form of our love of violence. To grow up in the South and other pockets of football love across America is as close to being raised in athletic Sparta as an American youth can experience. You are raised to play football, and no teenager ever played on a winning football team who did not consider himself one of life's chosen winners. Homecoming rituals are an affirmation of those values and the culture that honors the most American of sports.

When I was in high school and college, I'd imagined myself far too cool to enjoy the simple pleasures of homecoming rituals. This strikes me now not as hip or enlightened but as a reflection of some deeper insecurity. I wasn't confident enough in who I was or might become, so I was afraid of being limited by embracing the traditional. It was like a self-impressed atheist who steers away from churches for fear of being converted. But now none of that mattered, and maybe coming back to it at this stage in my life made it better.

The night before homecoming game, Ole Miss has a parade that starts on campus and ends up at the square of Oxford, a little over a mile away. The proximity of town to campus is one of the special pleasures of Oxford, a connection grown stronger with the explosion of clubs and bars.

"If Oxford had been like this," my father said as students jammed the square, "I'm not sure I would have graduated."

"If I had known Oxford was like this," I said, "I would have come here and never left."

Earlier there had been student elections for homecoming: Miss Ole Miss, Mr. Ole Miss, homecoming maids who now rolled by in convertibles, waving. From the bars and balconies of clubs, cheers rang out. The whole scene had just enough self-awareness to laugh a bit at itself. Yes, all this is old-fashioned and retro, but it's fun and nobody is taking it that seriously. We were in front of Square Books, where my mother had disappeared for most of the afternoon. Earlier I'd found a book in its extensive civil rights/southern collection detailing the history of race murders in Mississippi, *Devil's Sanctuary*. It was full of photographs of lynching and detailed accounts of young black men killed for the supposed crime of looking at white women, or whistling, as with the Emmett Till horror.

The year before, an African American woman had been homecoming queen, and this crowd was black and white, spilling out of the clubs together. Those segregationists who had railed against "Negro music" and the dangers of allowing black athletes onto the playing field with white boys had lost the day more than their worst nightmares might have conjured.

From a balcony bar, a pack of sorority girls cheered, "Mash those Idaho potatoes!"

My father winced. "It's just . . ."

"Lame," I said.

"Lame," he agreed.

My mother came out of Square Books with a load of books so large they seemed to be pulling her down to the sidewalk.

"What's lame?" she asked.

"Drunk sorority girls yelling, 'Mash those Idaho potatoes.'"

"I know they weren't Kappas," she said, handing me the stack of books. "But if Ole Miss can't beat Idaho, it will be sad."

For Ole Miss, playing Idaho was about picking an opponent they were likely to beat on homecoming. For Idaho, it was about the experience of playing in the SEC. And money. A lot of money.

Idaho made $850,000 playing Ole Miss that Saturday evening. The yearly revenue for Idaho's entire football season was a little over $5 million, including television fees and ticket sales. So the one trip down south made up almost 20 percent of the year's budget and twice what would be made from a year's worth of tickets.

Why was it worth it to Ole Miss to pay just under $1 million? A single home game for an SEC team generates an average of around $4 million in total revenue, from ticket sales, concessions, and broadcast revenues. Even sharing $850,000 with an opponent, Ole Miss made money playing the Idaho game.

Smaller "programs," as they are invariably called, like Idaho are known in football parlance as cupcakes. They are on the schedule to increase the odds the team will win enough games to qualify for a bowl game and to give a respite from the grueling intensity of SEC play. In 2013, the Ole Miss schedule had been ranked one of the most difficult in the nation, so it seemed fair that the team should have a bite or two of a cupcake.

Of course sometimes it just doesn't work out. A month after the Ole Miss–Idaho game, the University of Florida, one of the great SEC programs going through a rough stretch, lost to small Georgia Southern at home in the infamous "Swamp." This prompted the cruel and perfect headline GATORS CHOKE ON A CUPCAKE.

But against the Idaho Vandals, Ole Miss didn't choke. About halfway through the first half, the head football writer for the *Clarion Ledger,* Hugh Kellenberger, tweeted, "Idaho is not a very good football team." It was a bit of an understatement. Ole Miss led 17–0 at the end of the first quarter, but it wasn't really the score that was so telling. It was the way they did it, like a cat playing with a mouse. They didn't seem to be trying that hard. When Ole Miss scored twenty-one points in the third quarter to lead 45–7, we thought it was safe to leave. "I think we got this one in the bag," Dad said. "What do you say we go back to your mother?"

In the elevator down, Dad grinned broadly. "I'm ready for Arkansas next week." He tilted his head back slightly toward the ceiling of the elevator. "Pig Sooie!" he cried, letting go the Arkansas battle cry.

"The Hogs are tough," I said.

"The Hogs are tough."

9

····

The first Ole Miss–Arkansas football game was in 1908. They hadn't played every year since, but this was the fifty-ninth game, which wasn't bad as far as American sports rivalries went. A sociologist or political scientist would most likely posit that the game had taken on an unusual intensity given the sad economic conditions of both states. Mississippi was usually at the bottom when it came to the standard measurements of just how many different ways a society could fail economically. But Arkansas was right there next to us to offer comfort and occasionally, in good years, would dip below Mississippi.

But when I was a kid, none of that had mattered. Then it was just about hogs. To be surrounded by the lurid spectacle of grown men and women wearing plastic pigs on their heads and howling "Woo Pig Sooie!" must have been what it was like to be young and Roman and witness normally staid adults at the Colosseum howling for blood. There is a picture of Bill Clinton in his twenties with one of those big hog hats on his head at a game, grinning madly. He looks ecstatic. Can anyone doubt for a second that had he been given the gifts and the chance, Bill Clinton would have much preferred to be a starting all-American football player at the University of Arkansas than a Rhodes scholar? What better way for a young male desperate for glory with a love of women and a deep need to impress his mother to prove he was more than the fat kid in the Bubba jeans (as Bill Clinton once described his childhood) than running through the tunnel as a Razorback to the roar of tens of thousands of hog-hat-wearing maniacs? Woo Pig Sooie!

Arkansas football had been going through a rough time ever since a spring day in 2012 when their star coach, Bobby Petrino, slid his motorcycle off a country road not far from the university in Fayetteville. He'd broken four ribs, cracked a vertebra, and appeared at a press conference the next day in a neck brace looking as if he had been dragged behind a truck down one of those rough Arkansas roads politicians are always promising to improve. The sympathy his condition generated evaporated like a heat mirage when it soon came out that a beautiful former volleyball player who was now on the athletic department payroll had been on the back of his motorcycle. It wasn't just that the married Petrino was having an affair with a blonde as tall as he was. It wasn't just that he first lied about her being in the wreck to the police and university officials. It wasn't just that he had recently "lent" her $20,000. It wasn't just that he had hired her in the athletic department, so he was now having an affair with an employee. Any one or two of these for a coach with Petrino's record—he had taken the Razorbacks from losers to an 11-2 record the year before and the promise of an SEC or national championship on the horizon—might have been survivable. It was the combination that killed the guy. The Arkansas athletic director cried when he announced Petrino's firing a few days after the accident. Not a football fan in Arkansas thought those were tears for Petrino. Those were tears for the games this entire mess might have cost the Hogs.

The drama of big-name and big-dollar coaches has become a standard trope in college football, and it only seems natural that the biggest dramas would be on college football's brightest stage, the SEC. Before Bobby Petrino, Arkansas had gone through a boom-and-bust cycle with another coach, Houston Nutt. He was an Arkansas boy whose parents had taught at the Arkansas School for the Deaf in Little Rock, where his dad was athletic director and head basketball coach. Growing up with a burning dream to play quarterback for the Razorbacks, Nutt had been the last player recruited by Arkansas's legendary coach, Frank Broyles. Broyles was the Bear Bryant of Arkansas. Nutt was a classic drop-back quarterback and so talented he started four games as a freshman, but Broyles's replacement, Lou Holtz, favored an option-style offense and moved him to second string. He ended up transferring from Arkansas to Oklahoma State, as bitter a parting as breaking up with your first real girlfriend.

Houston Nutt played basketball and football at Oklahoma State but never became a star. He went into coaching and turned a series of lesser programs at Murray State and Boise State into winners. That brought him back to Arkansas in 1997 as head coach, riding into Fayetteville the returning prodigal son. In his first press conference, he predicted the Hogs would win a national championship. The Razorbacks, including one of their greatest fans in the White House, went crazy.

It proved to be a tortured, high-intensity love affair. A fanatical Arkansas fan who thought that Nutt wasn't doing enough for the Hogs filed a Freedom of Information request for the phone records of his university-issued cell phone. Amazingly, he got them. Then he released them to the press. That let the Arkansas fan base know that their beloved coach had placed more than a thousand calls and text messages to an attractive female sports announcer at a small Arkansas television station. There was also a problem that a family friend of Nutt's sent an e-mail to Arkansas's star quarterback, who sometimes seemed not to be too excited about playing at Arkansas, urging the kid to quit. Which he promptly did, transferring to another school, leaving Nutt to explain what in the world was a friend of his doing running off one of the team's star players. All of this made for high drama that became operatic in 2007 when Nutt announced that he was resigning from Arkansas and then a few hours later announced he was taking the head coaching job at Ole Miss. In college football, this was like the president of the United States announcing he was resigning and then turning up a Canadian premier a few hours later. Ole Miss fans were ecstatic, and part of the joy was stealing him from Arkansas. At Ole Miss, he had a few good years, then a couple of disastrous seasons that led to his firing in 2011 and Hugh Freeze. In his last season at Ole Miss, Nutt did not win a single SEC game and hasn't coached since.

Arkansas fans loved and valued football, and that was important. For the rivalry to have a truly desperate quality, it needed to be valued equally by both sides. The Sharks and the Jets must hate each other with matching passion. Football was important enough to Arkansans and Mississippians to make the intensity around the games seem the proper natural order.

The rituals of the Ole Miss–Arkansas game energized my father. There had been something unsettling about playing a team like Idaho. What possible glory was there in defeating a team that played in a conference that no one could name? All SEC football fans believe that non-SEC teams are suspect and played a version of the game that, even if played well, could not satisfy a true football fan. The University of Oregon may turn out superb football teams, but they have a fondness for Nike-sponsored garish uniforms that resemble synchronized swimming outfits, and, really, how serious can you get about a stadium full of fans screaming for the . . . Ducks? In Idaho, Boise State had produced some terrific teams, but they were most famous for playing on a blue field. Blue. My God. A partial dispensation could be granted to members of the Southwest Conference, of which Arkansas, Texas, and Texas A&M had been members. But in recent years, Texas A&M and Arkansas had seen the light and come over to the true faith, joining the SEC.

"The Hogs take their football seriously," my father said over breakfast after the Idaho game, and I joined in with what I knew would be next. "The Hogs are tough." He looked at me, smiling.

"That's just what you used to say before the Arkansas games back when," I said to my dad: "The Hogs are tough."

We were eating at Alumni House, with a mix of hungover fans and young recruits with their families who had come in for the game. Across the way, Coach Hugh Freeze was eating with two young players, one white, one black, and their families. He was wearing his Ole Miss warm-up suit, and the players had the nervous pleasure of being in the presence of a celebrity.

Around the room were young sons having breakfast with their fathers, and I wondered if they were hearing the same, looking forward to next week: The Hogs are tough. Gonna be a good game. After breakfast, we went for a walk around the

Grove as the tents of the night before were dismantled and the green space returned, until the next Friday night at 9:00 when it would happen again.

"I think I started falling in love with football around these Arkansas games," I told my father. "They always seemed like such a big deal. Those parties you and Mom would have, the hog roasts. I don't think people have parties like that before baseball games."

"It was fun," he said simply. "After the Depression, the war, coming back. I think we liked parties even more. People wanted to be happy. And that was hard sometimes. A lot of us were just glad to be alive after the war. We wanted to have families, get back to normal."

"So let me ask you something I've always wondered," I said. "We talk about the greatest generation now, but when you were going through all this, did it feel that way?" We walked on for a bit before he answered.

"No, not at all, really. We'd all seen the Depression and how people coped with that disaster, just the day to day to get by. That was so hard. Some people just broke. Families broke. My parents went through that, raised a big family. That was something."

"But you went to war, came back and"—I shrugged—"started over. That's amazing."

"Everybody went to war. And when everybody went to war, it didn't seem special that you did it. It was just what everybody did."

"Did you ever regret leaving the FBI and going into the navy? You could have stayed in the FBI."

After graduating from law school, he had entered the FBI and ended up in New York City, watching mostly German nationals or Americans with ties to Germany as possible spies. When I lived in Manhattan, I could call him for subway advice on how to get to obscure points in the city, and he would usually nail the connections. He lived with a couple of other Mississippians on the Upper West Side, went to plays and sports events at every chance, and fell in love with the city. He still loved it.

He shook his head. "I started having friends who were getting killed or wounded. I couldn't sit there while they were overseas. And think what I would have felt like when Francis was wounded, if I was still sitting in New York." His younger brother, Francis, was terribly wounded in Europe and missing in action for months before word came that he was alive and in a German POW hospital. He went on to a great career in civil rights law but never completely recovered from the machine-gun attack, walking a little crookedly the rest of his life. Like many vets, he didn't like to talk about his experiences, but when I turned twenty-one, he wrote me an extraordinary letter saying that his experiences in war compelled him to pursue civil justice for a career and urged me to follow my passions in life. I still read the letter regularly, never without questioning whether I had followed his advice. He developed early dementia in part from the head wound he received in the war. At his funeral a few years earlier, I wished desperately that I had spent more time with him before he slipped away.

"When Uncle Francis went into civil rights work, did you ever think of leaving the firm and following him?"

"I wanted to build the firm. It was right for him, but I was always really proud of what he did." He looked away and started to tear up. "He had a really big heart. I miss him a lot."

"So do I." He thought for a moment and smiled.

"I miss Aunt Ebby and Aunt White too." He called them "aunt" because that's how I knew his two older sisters. They were extraordinary women; both had graduate degrees and taught on university levels. I remembered them as smart and ironic with a great love for their brother, my father, who had doted on them and provided a constant, steady presence in their lives just as he did for everyone. My dad had lost all his siblings now, and I tried to imagine what that was like. Two brothers had died when he was very young, one I was named for. He had lost his hero and older brother at forty not long after he got home from the Pacific. Of that once full house on North Street in Jackson, he was the only one left.

I loved the yearly Stevens Family Reunion held in Richton, the little town in southern Mississippi where my grandfather had been born and many relatives lived. Somewhere along the way, that died out, and though my sister lived not far away in Laurel, Mississippi, those boisterous gatherings of dinner on the grounds on blistering summer days seemed long ago. When I wondered if I should have had children, it was mostly the notion that maybe more of that world, more of my mother and father, would have been passed on and lived a bit longer, if only in memory.

"I've been thinking about this a lot and have reached a conclusion," Dad announced as we turned the corner and the Vaught-Hemingway Stadium loomed in front of us.

"About?" I was still lost in thought about family reunions past.

"Ole Miss will beat Arkansas."

It was sunny and chilly on Saturday, the sort of day that made you start to miss summer. It had been a strange season, but then every season was strange in its own way. My dad and I walked—slowly, as always, a gait I was finally learning to adopt—across the Grove in the sunshine to the Arkansas game, feeling good about the prospects of our life over the next few hours. We'd learned that Ole Miss this year wasn't that "one in a million" miracle squad that would seize immortality. But they weren't bad either. They were good enough to make us confident that a sunny afternoon of autumn coolness wouldn't be ruined by the depression of unexpected defeat.

All of which explained the unease that washed over us when Arkansas took only six plays to score.

It was only a field goal, and the first possession of the game, but it felt terribly unjust and wrong to be denied even a few minutes to relax into the game. Every rational indicator pointed to the insignificance of such an early score: it was only three points and sort of a fluke at that. But this is not how a fan thinks. At least it wasn't how my father and I thought.

The bright afternoon seemed to grow darker and colder. Arkansas had just lost two games by seventy points, and now they had marched onto our home field and confidently knocked out a score. "I don't like this," I said to my dad, staring glumly at the field, as if I could rewind the moment and will the field goal wide left.

"Well, it was a pretty lucky kick," Dad said of the long Arkansas field goal.

"But what if they're lucky all afternoon?"

He stared hard at the field, not answering, but there really wasn't a good answer. Ole Miss had considerably more talent on the field than Arkansas and were playing at home and should have taken control of the game early in the same way Alabama dominated Ole Miss. But instead the two teams slugged it out more or less equally for most of the first half. Because Ole Miss was the better team, they looked the worse of the two, playing under their level while the Razorbacks seemed eager for an upset. Arkansas's new coach, Bret Bielema, had great success at the University of Wisconsin and was accustomed to winning. Arkansas had gone through a rough stretch, but if their coach had convinced them that this was their game of destiny, the day they would turn it all around, they could be dangerous. Every team in the SEC has the talent, given the right combination of factors, to beat any other team.

With three minutes to go in the half, Ole Miss led by three points, stopped on the one-yard line by a furious Arkansas goal line stand. As if fearing to go into the locker room and face their coach when leading by only three points, Ole Miss scored again. That made it 20–10, which did feel more like what we had expected, at least enough to make the halftime less anxious.

"Let's walk around a little," Dad suggested, surprising me. In all the games we'd been to this year, we'd never strayed far during the half.

"You sure?"

"You tired?" he asked, motioning for me to follow him. We made it around to the Arkansas side, a swirl of red and variations on the classic hog head. We got a couple of hot dogs and were leaning up against the stadium when a couple of Arkansas undergraduates walked by holding hands. He was a big guy, about six five, in an Arkansas baseball hat, and she was barely five feet under one of the largest hog hats I'd ever seen. My father smiled.

She stopped, pulling on her boyfriend's hand, cocked her head, and then wagged her finger at my father. "I know you're just jealous. You wish you had one of these."

"Absolutely!" Dad said, and it sounded as if he really meant it.

She took it off and held it out to my dad.

"I couldn't. It looks better on you. And it just doesn't go with the shirt." He nodded down to his Ole Miss shirt.

She nodded gravely in agreement.

"You know, I just feel sorry for you guys."

"Sorry?"

"I mean, you can't do the Colonel Reb thing anymore. And what in the world are you going to do with a black bear?"

The Black Bear was the mascot that was being suggested as the alternative to Colonel Reb. No one seemed to like it, and no one really understood it. Supposedly, it was a reference to Faulkner's story "The Bear," but that seemed only to prove why few mascots are named for stories written by Nobel Prize winners.

"The Bear," my father said, shaking his head.

"There you go," she said, smiling, raising her glass in a toast. "Hotty Toddy."

"Hotty Toddy," we both said.

"I like the hog heads," Dad said as they walked off, "but I'd be damned if I'd ever wear one."

"Humiliating," I agreed.

"I guess next year this game is at Arkansas?"

I nodded. "Yep. Fayetteville."

He nodded. "I don't know how many more of these Hog fests I have left in me." He smiled wistfully. This was something that had gone unspoken, that maybe these games were our last time together, surrounded by hog heads and Rebels and yelling our hearts out for young men on the field.

"It's a long drive to Fayetteville," I said. "And that stadium is always terrible, all those maniacs yelling 'Pig Sooie!'"

"Terrible," he agreed.

"But I tell you what," I said, putting my arm around him. "I'd love to go to any game with you anywhere. Anytime."

"Even Arkansas?"

"You bet."

"I'd like that," he said, giving my shoulder a squeeze. "I'd like that a lot."

We had hoped that Ole Miss would prove quickly in the second half why they were a heavy favorite to win. It would have been typical for a team with less talent, like Arkansas, to play an emotional first half and then, as if honor defended, tank in the last two quarters. But it didn't seem that's what Arkansas had in mind.

On the third play of the second half, Arkansas intercepted Bo Wallace on the Ole Miss forty-six-yard line. Four plays later, Arkansas scored. That made it 20–17. As my father and I were trying to convince ourselves that there was still good reason to think the afternoon was not tilting to disaster, Ole Miss scored.

The rest of the game wasn't pretty, but the Rebels managed to win, 34–24. We walked slowly back across campus. The Arkansas fans seemed to be taking defeat in good humor, but then they'd had a lot of practice the past couple of years. It was chilly, with the early sunset of daylight savings still coming as a surprise. "You know there's a party back at the hotel we're invited to," Dad said.

I didn't, but it wasn't a surprise. There were always lots of parties at the Inn at Ole Miss on the football weekends. "Hog roast," he said.

That sounded perfect. "Nothing beats a good hog roast," I said.

We both walked a little faster.

10

There were three games left in the season, but there was no pretending to value the games equally. First was Troy, which would be significant only if Ole Miss lost, and then it would rank as a great embarrassment. Next was Missouri, which was having one of those miracle seasons, losing only one game to South Carolina in a double overtime. They were ranked number eight in the country. And to beat them would signal that Ole Miss might have moved closer to the rarefied elite category, but there was no long history to an Ole Miss versus Missouri rivalry, and the game had little emotional resonance.

The season, like so many before, really came down to the last game, the one that really mattered, against Mississippi State: the Egg Bowl. Ole Miss and State had played 108 times since 1901. When I was growing up in Jackson, it was traditional to play the game on neutral turf at Memorial Stadium, and we never missed a game.

We spent those three weeks on campus, at the Alumni House. We had big rooms next to each other and continued the comfortable routine we'd fallen into over the fall. I'd get up early, go for a run, then come back and knock on my parents' door. We'd sit around and drink coffee and talk, mostly about what news there was in the family. My sister's kids were living in New York now and dealing with the ups and downs of life after college.

A nephew of my dad's, one of my favorite cousins, was going through a rough health patch. And we talked about my parents moving full-time to New Orleans, instead of dividing their time between Asheville and New Orleans. My mother always loved to "just explore options" on pretty much anything, from vacations to college courses she was thinking of auditing to where they should live. I suspect it came from years in Jackson in a world where options were limited and it was a mental escape to consider all the possibilities of various changes. My father was much more linear: let's decide what to do and do it, and he tended to be comfortable with whatever road was taken. He was not one to second-guess.

Once these options had been, in theory at least, pretty much limitless: What about studying Spanish in Mexico or renting an apartment in New York or volunteering to teach for a year in a school? My mother had a deep interest in the world and passed the Gore Vidal test that to be interesting you had to be interested. She was interested in anything and everything.

The choices my mother mused about were more limited now that time no longer stretched without visible horizons. I had thought it made sense for her and Dad to stay at the Methodist retirement center in Asheville, which was a good and decent place with a built-in infrastructure for anticipated needs. But my mother had let slip something in passing that stopped me cold. "I don't want to die here," she said, and after that I just shut up and stayed out of the decision. It made the choice so basic and primal that I felt I had no standing to voice an opinion. It was about not convenience or odds but something very basic and stark and private.

All along, the football season had been just an excuse to

spend time together, and now that we were toward the end of the season, it seemed less important to pretend the games were really the best moments. It had been a good season if not a magical one, but a reminder that while it was inevitable to long for perfect seasons, they grace us rarely, if ever, and that was okay.

The two rooms where we gathered in the mornings seemed to reflect how our lives had changed. My parents had built a house on a dead-end street to raise my sister and me, a world that had seemed as a child to be sprawling and filled with hidden spaces where I could slip away and lose myself in dreams of life's adventures waiting to be seized. I'd climb up into the attic or down in the basement or even duck behind a big couch in the living room and read for hours. One of my favorite discoveries, passed down from my father, was the Memphis writer Richard Haliburton. His *Royal Road to Romance* was the story of traveling around the world, climbing the Matterhorn, swimming in the Taj Mahal reflecting pool, drinking from life like a big, overflowing cup. I'd wanted all those sorts of adventures so much that I would stay up all night willing myself to grow up faster so I could begin to live that life. Over the years, I had found ways to do many of those things, and now that big house of my youth, which was really never that big, was gone, and it was just me and my parents in a couple of rooms at the Ole Miss Alumni House. But the chance to be together seemed as important as any Swiss climb or African adventure.

Every morning after we sat around and drank coffee, Dad would eventually ask, "What do you think about breakfast?" as if it were really a question. We always ate breakfast. Then we'd go for a walk around campus, not very far, and back to the hotel. And so the days unwound.

At some point in almost every day, I'd find myself thinking about what life had been like a year earlier, when the campaign had been so crazy. The one-year anniversary of the election came, and I celebrated it with my longest run of the fall, about twenty slow miles. I still felt a deep sense of personal failure that I was beginning to understand might never disappear. The goal was to elect a president, and I had failed. I'd discovered it was almost impossible to discuss the campaign with anyone who hadn't been part of it or another presidential. What side someone had been on mattered less than the shared experience, and I imagined, without really knowing, that it might be close to what cops or firefighters or those in the military experienced. It was such an intense, pressured, chaotic process that demanded so much it was inevitable that one began and ended a different person. I no longer woke up in the middle of the night worried about the race, but there were still long periods when I'd lie in bed reading and trying, never very successfully, not to relive the campaign. By now, much had been written about the race, and inevitably much was wrong or half-right, and there were moments when I resolved to correct this inaccuracy or set the record straight about what really happened. But I knew at the end of the day, whatever I wrote, nothing would change the basic fact: we had lost. And that loss would never change.

I was jealous of the athletes we'd spent the autumn watching who could lose one weekend and go out and redeem themselves with a victory the next. It wasn't like that in presidential politics. I hadn't expected this, but being with my parents and watching them adjust to the changes that life brought was helping me understand the need to go forward. I couldn't change what had happened, but I could push ahead just as they were doing each day.

On warm afternoons, and there were still plenty of those left in Oxford, Dad and I would take a slow walk over to the football practice field next to the stadium. The high walls of the stadium loomed over the field, a dominant, brooding presence, reminding all of the urgency of the endeavor. In the fading light of the late afternoons, it seemed impossibly quiet, as if the intensity of the previous Saturday had forced the structure into exhausted silence. Standing just a few feet from the practice field, I found it easier to grasp the sheer athleticism of the players. Out of some routine moment, running pass routes or working in a new blitz, a player would suddenly explode in some minor miracle of grace and power. Sometimes it went unnoticed, even by coaches focused elsewhere, but at least a few times each practice a one-handed catch or a burst of speed as a back shot through an impossibly small hole untouched would be rewarded by shouts and laughing applause from players and coaches. "You see that . . . Man! . . . That was a Sunday play, sure thing."

Sunday play: NFL-level play—the ultimate compliment. Ole Miss had produced nearly three hundred NFL draft picks in its history, but it was nowhere near the top of the list; USC and Notre Dame had almost five hundred each. All schools liked to boast of their "athletic traditions," promising a unique experience for an athlete at the college. Alabama under Coach Nick Saban had elevated that to a straight monetary transaction: "$51,810,000.00," read the pitch Alabama sent to high school recruits. That was the amount of the contracts signed by the recent crop of Alabama NFL draftees. There were future NFL players on the Ole Miss practice field, but most would play their last game of big-time football in college.

"I hope they enjoy it," my father said one afternoon as we watched the players gather around Coach Hugh Freeze at the end of a practice. "It goes fast."

And it did. In that soft light of the late afternoon, I was once again a young boy on his way to the big game with his dad. It did go fast. But maybe for a moment or two, you could lean against life's spinning wheel and slow it just enough to savor the true pleasures of a fall afternoon, when young men who felt normal doing extraordinary things could be appreciated.

"Let's go find your mother," Dad said. "She'll be wondering where we are."

I nodded, shivering a little in the sudden cold of the setting sun.

That Saturday, Ole Miss set a team record of 751 offensive yards, beating Troy 51–21. It was a noon game on a day that was warm but would chill as soon as the sun dropped. It was one of those games when you could believe that all things were possible on a football field—until you stopped to think that it was Troy that Ole Miss was beating. They were a small university that hadn't started to play Division One football until 2001. Not that they couldn't be dangerous: they had defeated Mississippi State in their first Division One game and been to five bowl games over the last decade. But they were in a slump the past couple of years, and earlier in the season Mississippi State had crushed them

62–7. If you were looking for glory, there was little in defeating Troy this year.

But Missouri, the last home game of the season, would be a real test. The team was on a roll, playing with the confidence of a team who believed they had been sprinkled with fortune's gold dust. Game day was cold. Oxford was flooded with good-natured Missouri fans dressed in unfortunate combinations of gold and black, like so many bumblebees. "Something bothers me about these Missouri folks," I said to my dad as we walked through the Grove, stopping to see friends and eat along the way.

My father looked at me over a drumstick of delicious fried chicken that we had looted from a cousin's tent. "Come on," he said, "nice as can be." He gestured around. The Missouri fans in their black and gold stood out in a sea of Ole Miss red. Troy had been a blue day. They usually alternated. That I knew these things now pleased me greatly.

"That's what worries me," I said glumly.

He thought about it, then got it. "Yep. They're in too good a mood. They aren't nervous." We had seen this before at the Alabama game. It was not a good omen.

"We could just stay here and watch it on television," I said. There was a television in the tent. There were a lot of televisions around the Grove.

Dad looked horrified at the suggestion. "What would they do without us?" he asked.

I nodded. He was right.

"We can't miss the game," he said, waving his drumstick emphatically.

It was one of those games that are meant for drinking. Only

my dad and I weren't drinking. It was freezing cold, and Missouri scored on their first possession. The Ole Miss team looked uncomfortable in the chill, sluggish and out of sync. There was little of the grace and explosive spontaneity we'd seen at the practices. My father and I huddled under a blanket and looked at each other. He shrugged. I shrugged. We didn't move through the first half, when Missouri had methodically rolled to a 17–3 lead. "Hot dogs," Dad said. "Only hot dogs can make me feel better." I agreed and struggled up from under our blanket to return with a handful.

For a moment at the opening of the second half, it looked as if Ole Miss might rebound. They scored on four plays, making it 17–10. But it was false hope. Missouri quickly scored again, and then both teams seemed to just go through the motions, too cold to do much more than endure. The game ended with Missouri slowly moving down the field. Games that end when the winning team has the ball always feel unsatisfying. There's none of the frantic urgency of one team trying desperately to come back. It just ends.

We stood and stretched in a strangely quiet stadium. The Missouri fans had politely applauded, then fled the cold. The Ole Miss fans just headed for home, the Grove, and Oxford bars. We walked slowly back as I thought about how this was the final home game of the season and wished it had ended in some dazzling and joyful brilliance. "It's important to remember," Dad said, "particularly after a game like this: it's never too early to beat State."

That, of course, picked me up. "You're right, we have to focus on the positive. Beating State." He nodded.

"Go to hell, State," I said, like a catechism. "I feel better now."

He nodded. "That's right. Focus on the positive."

The Egg Bowl between Ole Miss and Mississippi State had nothing to do with eggs, and it wasn't, of course, really a bowl game. The name came from the trophy, which was basically a massive gold football that looked like, well, a big egg. It was created after a fight broke out in 1926 when Ole Miss students tried to tear down the goalposts in Starkville, home of Mississippi State, after Ole Miss won for the first time in thirteen years. An Ole Miss fraternity came up with the idea that fans might be less likely to attack each other with cane-bottom chairs—the weapon of choice in the 1926 brawl because they lined the field—if there was a formal exchange of a trophy. It seems a charmingly dated gesture of formality, like something from the British Raj, but it seemed to mostly work. In 1997, a fight broke out between the two teams before the game, but at least the fans didn't join in.

Mississippi State, originally called the Agricultural and Mechanical College of the State of Mississippi, was one of America's land-grant colleges. It was founded in 1878, so it wasn't haunted by a generation of students who died in a lost war. Like most of the land-grant versus state university rivalries around the country—Texas A&M versus University of Texas and Oklahoma State versus University of Oklahoma were classics—the working motif was that Ole Miss was full of entitled snobs and State was a cow college. Some time before World War II, State students embraced that image by bringing cowbells to the football games. I remembered vividly their obnoxious clanging from my first Ole Miss–State game.

In those days, it was just assumed that Ole Miss would win, and mostly they did. Starting in 1973, they played the game at Memorial Stadium in Jackson for fifteen straight years. The stadium was convenient neutral turf and would hold more fans than either Oxford or Starkville. Then both universities expanded their stadiums and returned to alternating venues.

This was a Starkville year.

We'd been invited to go to the game with a friend of my sister's. "She's a big Mississippi State fan," my sister, who was not a football fan, told me. "Her father loved the place, and they have season tickets."

This sounded great.

We were staying at a depressing little motel that was the last room we could find in town. The game was on Thanksgiving Day, which was more or less standard for the Egg Bowl, though sometimes they played it a day or two after, which seemed to make more sense to me. While my parents took a nap, I walked across the street to a grocery store. There is something particularly sad and forlorn about stores open on holidays like Thanksgiving. A few people ran around buying frozen turkey dinners, while others shopped as if it weren't a holiday. There was a huge display of Mississippi State swag, including the largest collection of cowbells I'd ever seen.

"You going to the game?" asked the smiling woman working the checkout. She was in her forties, and I could see an open copy of *The Lord of the Rings* tucked away behind the counter.

"You bet," I said.

She focused on my Ole Miss shirt and said, in a perfectly pleasant voice, "Go to hell, Ole Miss."

I laughed.

"You want a cowbell, don't you?" She leaned toward me and lightly thumped the Ole Miss logo on my shirt. "I know you do." For a moment, I thought about it. It might be sort of fun to have a big Mississippi State cowbell. I could picture it on my desk. I'd ring it when I was on conference calls that went too long and claim it was a fire alarm.

"Well," I said.

She shook her head. "Don't even think about it. I wouldn't sell it to you."

I smiled and laughed, but I don't think she was kidding.

Back at the hotel, we ate Chinese food my mother had ordered. The next day, we'd drive back to North Carolina and have a "real" Thanksgiving dinner with my sister's family over the weekend. While we ate off paper plates I'd been instructed to buy at the grocery—my mother would never consider eating out of a Chinese food container—we talked about the first Thanksgiving my parents had on their own, at a Manhattan Automat, where food was served from vending machines, a novelty in 1949. They had been married a week earlier and taken the train to New York to catch the SS *Queen of Bermuda* for a honeymoon cruise to Bermuda. The Automat story was a family staple I'd heard for years, but sitting in that chipped motel room in Starkville, I found its familiarity comforting. We had been through variations of the story for decades at Thanksgiving; now I appreciated there were Thanksgivings ahead when my parents wouldn't be here to share the story. There is a photograph of them on the deck of the *Queen of Bermuda* that my mother has displayed at every place they had ever lived. She had it in their room where we'd been staying at Ole Miss: she and my father, beautiful and hand-

Mom and Dad on their honeymoon,
Queen of Bermuda, 1949

some, leaning into a stiff wind, hair blowing, arm in arm, a lifetime stretching ahead of them with no horizons. Now, sixty-four years later, they were still together, once again eating a quirky Thanksgiving dinner, and if those horizons were much closer now and the shore within sight, their voyage had been, all in all, a good one. They had created a life together and brought my sister and me into their world.

"You know," I said, reaching for more of the bad egg rolls, "we're lucky. Susan and I are the luckiest kids in the world."

My mother smiled and came over and kissed my father and me lightly on the head. "We are lucky," she said. "All of us."

Nell Wade, my sister's friend, picked my dad and me up before the game. She was tall, wearing jeans, and she looked like somebody who loved to ride horses, which is how she and my sister became friends.

"You know all my crowd is die-hard State," she said, laughing. "I'm just warning you." She seemed to take her football with the proper seriousness, going through the lament of a fan after a difficult season as we drove to the stadium. By beating Arkansas in overtime the weekend before, State had eked out five of the mandatory six wins that is now established as the minimum for a team to be bowl eligible. But there had been close losses and blowouts, with enough flashes of talent to tantalize fans like Nell with the cruelest question in sports, if not life: What if?

"You know we almost beat Auburn," she said. "Just four points." That was the third game of the season, when no one realized Auburn would go undefeated and play in the national championship game. "And we did better against Alabama than you guys."

The game started at 7:30, but we had left early. "I don't want to rush your dad," Nell had said when we had talked earlier.

"We don't rush," I said, and it was true. "We're late sometimes, but we don't rush."

We weren't far from the campus, and in a couple of minutes the stadium was looming in the distance.

"Bigger than I remembered," Dad said.

"Oh, we expanded quite a bit. And still expanding. You know it's one of the oldest fields in the country," she said. "Not the stadium as it is, but they have been playing football here on this field since 1914."

Nell had a pass that let her drive almost all the way to the stadium. I assumed she wanted to drop off my dad and then go park. But to my astonishment, she pulled in to a parking space right next to the stadium.

"Like it," Dad said, never a fan of long walks from the car to the stadium.

We got out. If we had been any closer to the stadium, we would have been in one of the tunnels leading to the locker room. It was a small parking lot and had only a few cars.

"This is okay?" I asked.

She looked at me, puzzled.

"I mean, we can park here? This close?"

She nodded. "All good. Let's go watch my Dawgs crush the Rebels." She said it with the bloodlust of a true fan. It was one of those sunny days that would turn cold very fast when the sun went down, a repeat of the previous Saturday against Missouri. Ole Miss had played terribly in the cold, and a sudden pang of dread hit me.

"I'm worried about the cold," I announced, as if it were a profundity worth considering. "Ole Miss has played terribly when it's cold."

"I think," my father said, "the weather will be the same for both teams."

We followed Nell into the stadium, where everyone seemed to know her. "We're up there," she said, pointing skyward. There was a ramp that wound around the outside leading to the upper decks. "But let's take the elevator. I can't walk that far," she said with a laugh.

"If you insist," Dad said.

We got off on the top level, arranged much like the Ole Miss stadium, a hallway lined with the doors to skyboxes.

My father raised his eyebrows. "Fancy," he said.

Nell opened the door to the largest skybox I'd ever seen. It was on two levels, with windows that opened out on the field. We were precisely on the fifty-yard line.

My father did a double take. The design of the box gave the sensation of being unusually close to the field. We both looked over at Nell. She shrugged.

"It was what my dad wanted," she said, looking almost embarrassed by the gargantuan box.

"Your dad?" I asked.

Nell then told us how her father had loved Mississippi State, even though he had never attended. He had grown up on a farm, never graduated from college, and appreciated the agricultural roots of Mississippi State and its heritage as a land-grant university. He had gone on to make a fortune in insurance, turning a Georgia-based company into what became Aflac insurance.

"He loved State and decided to give it a lot of money," she said matter-of-factly. "His last big donation was for the stadium. So the family has this." She gestured around the vast skybox.

"Well," I said, not really knowing what to say.

"I just love the Dawgs, got that from my dad, and was happy to sit in the old stadium freezing on a night like this. But it made my dad happy to do this, and," she said, smiling, "it's not so bad."

Nell's family and friends, all rabid State fans, filtered into the box before kickoff, arriving with their dreaded cowbells. They regarded my father and me with a touch of benevolent regret, as if saddened that we had strayed from the true way of being a State fan.

"I am so sorry," one friend of Nell's announced, as if learning we had suffered some grievous wrong, "that you have to go through life with that Ole Miss burden."

The game never felt right from the start. Ole Miss had that sluggish, chilled look of the Missouri game. Position by position, they were a much better team and should have dominated. But they played tentatively, as if unsure of their own prowess. They didn't need to play over their heads to win, but they were definitely playing under their heads. At the half, it was tied 7–7, and though Ole Miss was the better team, Mississippi State had played better football. "One of my rules," Dad said, "is that it's always dangerous to let a team you should beat think they can win. It's like a court case. If you have the better case and don't take control early, it can be a disaster."

"Y'all don't look so happy," Nell teased. "Eat something." An elaborate spread had appeared in the back of the box: steamed shrimp, sliced steak, hot dogs, and hamburgers. I filled two plates full, and my father and I both attacked the plates as if they held the secret to winning the game.

At the start of the third quarter, Ole Miss came out with more intensity and focus, moving eighty-seven yards in a long seventeen-play drive. But they were stopped close to the goal and had to settle for a field goal that felt like a failure. Seventeen plays for three points? I looked at my dad, who was shaking his head.

Both teams continued to play oddly lackluster football, as if the cold and the long season had sapped their spark. In the fourth quarter, with the score tied 10–10, Mississippi State replaced their quarterback with Dak Prescott, their star, who had sat out the last few games with an injury. It was one of those moments that have a predictably scripted feel to them: wounded player comes off bench to be a hero. I instantly felt a sense of dread and deep unfairness. "That kid is hurt," I said to Dad, trying my best to sound concerned. "It's really wrong for him to be playing."

My father looked at me for a moment, then patted my knee. "Nice try."

While around us the State faithful cheered, Prescott ran or passed with enough dazzling moves to evoke unpleasant flashbacks of Johnny Manziel. With two seconds left in the game, he put Mississippi State on the Ole Miss twenty-one-yard line. The field goal team came out while our new Mississippi State friends grew pensively silent.

"Our kicker is terrible," Nell said. "Lord. Please."

I immediately felt better. "There's hope," I whispered to my father but still couldn't bring myself to watch the kick. When I heard Nell and her friends cry out in pain, my fan heart leaped with joy. Dad and I beamed at each other, then immediately felt guilty, as if we had insulted our hosts' cooking. "I saw you," Nell said, sighing. "It's okay. This is just when I have to remind myself it's only a game."

"Does that ever work?" Dad asked.

"Never," she said, sighing loudly. "Not once."

We were in overtime play, a concept I find insulting. For decades, college football games ended in ties, and no one thought it was a shameful state of affairs. Frustrating and disappointing, but it was a legitimate end to any contest: if after four quarters the score was a tie, the game ended in a tie. But then came this abominable "innovation" that forced teams to play a bastard-ized version of the game that was all too close to one of those shameful soccer shoot-outs.

My overtime hatred ramped up when Mississippi State won the toss and Dak Prescott quickly scored. The cowbells erupted. It was awful. My dad looked pained but stoic. He leaned forward, as if he could will the Rebels to score.

When Ole Miss started, they completed two quick passes to move to the eleven-yard line. "That's perfect," Dad said. "They can get a first down on the one-yard line."

Then, in one of those slow-motion nightmares, the quarterback Bo Wallace faked a handoff, then ran through a huge opening on the right side of the line. A couple of steps from the goal line, a Mississippi State defender desperately lunged for Wallace, missing the tackle but knocking the ball from his arms. "No!" my father yelled, jumping to his feet as I followed him.

As the ball skidded into the end zone, Wallace reached out for it without a chance in the world to bring it back as Mississippi State recovered, winning the game. Bo Wallace lay where he had fallen, and all I could think about was how horrible he must feel. It was the last game of the year, and this is how it ended. "That was . . ." I struggled to find the right word.

"Cruel," Dad said. I nodded.

Nell came over and hugged us both. "I'm so sorry," she said, then laughed. "Okay, not really sorry, but I feel terrible for you!"

"Well," Dad said, sighing, "we've lost before."

On the way back to the hotel, we found ourselves behind the Ole Miss team bus. "Long ride back to Oxford," Dad said quietly.

Over the weekend, when we did the usual Thanksgiving thing

in North Carolina, Dad and I replayed the Egg Bowl game in all the different ways Ole Miss could have won. But in the end, after we had Wallace passing instead of fumbling into the end zone, after we had made the field goals that were missed, it came back to the same: we lost.

What Dad had said that night was true: we had lost before and would again. Somehow it seemed right that it was a loss of a different sort, a political campaign, that had led me into one more season. Both had ended on cold November nights with much regret. But I was learning that at the end of the day there was the end of the day and loss awaits us all. There might have been a time when I thought great success could freeze time or buy a little piece of something close to immortality, but that was, I realized, vain foolishness. Like this season my father and I just had, there would always be losses, and they would always hurt, but there was still the time together and shared joys.

"I think they'll be better next year," Dad said. We were sitting on the couch at my sister's house, watching some Thanksgiving weekend games that didn't interest us much.

For an hour or so, we went through all the reasons that Ole Miss would improve: third year of Coach Hugh Freeze, Bo Wallace would have more experience, the incredible freshmen would be sophomores.

"Do you believe it?" I asked my father.

"Of course!" he responded instantly. Then smiled. "You have to believe it's going to be better, don't you?"

I agreed.

"Let's go outside," he said.

We both bundled up, and on the way out the door he picked

up an old football that was sitting in a corner. One of my sister's dogs liked to push it around with his nose.

Outside my dad bounced it up and down in his hands, then nodded to me. "Go long," he said.

I trotted across her lawn. He got between the imaginary center's legs, took the snap, and dropped back a few feet to pass. He threw the wobbly spiral over my head. I shouted and chased the ball.

"Run," Dad yelled. "You got it."

I caught it, then turned to toss it to him.

"Next year will be better," I said.

He caught the ball with surprising grace. Somewhere in there was still a true athlete.

"No doubt about it," he said and lofted the ball toward me.

I ran to catch it.

A NOTE ABOUT THE AUTHOR

Stuart Stevens grew up in Jackson, Mississippi. He has worked in many political campaigns in the United States and abroad. The author of five previous books, he has also written extensively for television, including *Northern Exposure*. His writing has been published in *The New York Times, The Washington Post, Esquire, Outside,* and *The Atlantic,* among others. He is a columnist for The Daily Beast. For more information, visit www.stuartstevens.com.

A NOTE ON THE TYPE

This book was set in Legacy Serif. Ronald Arnholm (b. 1939) designed the Legacy family after being inspired by the 1470 edition of *Eusebius* set in the roman type of Nicolas Jenson. This revival type maintains much of the character of the original. Its serifs, stroke weights, and varying curves give Legacy Serif its distinct appearance. It was released by the International Typeface Corporation in 1992.

Composed by North Market Street Graphics,
Lancaster, Pennsylvania

Printed and bound by Berryville Graphics,
Berryville, Virginia

Designed by M. Kristen Bearse